GOD'S ACRES

DAVID GERARD

DIAMOND MEDIA PRESS CO.
1-304-273-6157
https://www.diamondmediapressco.com/

Copyright © 2021

By David Gerard
All rights reserved.

No part of this book may be used or reproduced by any means, graphic, electronic, or mechanical, including photocopying, recording, taping or by any information storage retrieval system without the written permission of the author except in the case of brief quotations embodied in critical articles and reviews.

The views expressed in this work are solely those of the author and do not necessarily reflect the views of the publisher, and the publisher hereby disclaims any responsibility for them.

No part of this book may be reproduced in any form or by any electronic

or mechanical means including information storage and retrieval systems, without permission, in writing from the author. The only exception is by the reviewer, who may quote short excerpts in a review.

Any people depicted in stock imagery provided by Thinkstock are models,

and such images are being used for illustrative purposes only. Certain stock imagery @Thinkstock.

ISBN Paperback: 978-195130275-7

"To Bill, whose memories and encouragement helped this book along"

April 26, 2011

Pen Ultimate Press
Winnie Sullivan
520 N Skinker Boulevard
St. Louis, MO 63130

Dear Winnie,

Congratulations on winning the 2011 Oklahoma Center for the Book Award in the fiction category for *God's Acres*, by David Gerard.

Enclosed is the publisher's medal. I have also enclosed a copy of the press release listing the finalists and the winners as well as a few award stickers. Feel free to reproduce these on those winning books if you desire, or if you wish to purchase additional stickers they are $.20 each.

Best wishes on the continued success of this book. Please keep the Oklahoma Center for the Book and the Oklahoma Book Awards in mind for future promotion of books featuring Oklahoma or Oklahoma authors.

Please call me if you need any further information at 405/522-3383 or email carmstrong@oltn.odl.state.ok.us.

Respectfully,

Connie G. Armstrong
Executive Director

Contents

Introit One 1
    Chapter One 3
Introit Two 15
    Chapter Two 17
Introit Three 27
    Chapter Three 29
Introit Four 41
    Chapter Four 43
Introit Five 53
    Chapter Five 55
Introit Six 67
    Chapter Six 69
Introit Seven 81
    Chapter Seven 83
Introit Eight 95
    Chapter Eight 97
Introit Nine 107
    Chapter Nine 109
Introit Ten 119
    Chapter Ten 121
Introit Eleven 131
    Chapter Eleven 133
Introit Twelve 149
    Chapter Twelve 151

Introit One

And the Lord God took man, and put him into the paradise of pleasure, to dress it, and to keep it. And he commanded him, saying: Of every tree of paradise thou shalt eat: But of the tree of knowledge of good and evil, thou shalt not eat. For in what day soever thou shalt eat of it, thou shalt die the death.

— Genesis 2: 15b-17, Douay-Rheim Version of the Bible

My mother lay dying, three hundred miles away.

My sister Janice feared Mom suffered.

But death is not always the greatest agony.

Years ago, when my mother was in her forties

— and I was a young child —

My mother experienced something worse than death.

Chapter One

IN JANUARY 1958, AFTER orbiting Earth for three months, Sputnik I fell from the sky.

At the end of January, the United States put its first satellite, Explorer 1, in orbit.

In a more heavenly move, in February, Pope Pius XII declared St. Clare the patron saint of television.

Television today, with its cable and satellite networks transmitting many crude, sensual and inane programs, must embarrass poor Clare. If heaven can be blamed for man's failures, then Clare must share in the blame for television's social degeneracy.

In March 1958, a U.S. bomber accidentally dropped an atom bomb on Mars Bluff, South Carolina. The conventional explosives in the bomb destroyed a house and injured a family.

No one died. The nuclear device was not inside the bomb, but still in the plane.

Nuclear weapons didn't have a patron saint in those days. That was good. Saints attract demons.

We must be careful now. In 2005, the Orthodox Church named the nineteenth-century Russian Admiral Fyodor Ushakov the patron saint of nuclear-armed, long-distance Russian bombers, so nuclear weapons have a patron saint, if only for the Orthodox.

The Orthodox must have thought that a patron saint of nuclear weapons would offer a measure of divine sanity after living four and a half decades under the earthly, restraining policy of mutual assured destruction and the building of thousands of nuclear bombs.

Who can figure out the Orthodox? They are a different breed.

My dad, a Ukrainian Catholic, was a strange blend of Orthodox and Roman. As baffling as he may have been in makeup, though, he was the only unconfused person in my family, and he was the only one prepared for the folly of what we would do in March 1958.

That was the month and year we moved to the farm, twelve acres of rich soil deposited over eons by the flooding of Contrary Creek. The creek wound out of a narrow valley that led into the much wider valley of the Missouri River.

The valley of Contrary Creek was not much different from the multitude of small valleys harbored within the low hills of northwest Missouri that border the Missouri River floodplain. But the valley of Contrary Creek, beginning in March 1958, held our twelve acres a few miles south of St. Joseph.

The acreage had belonged to a county judge. He sold it to my dad.

Mom thought that she talked Dad into buying it. But she – and we – only learned of Dad's motivation later.

Mom wanted a farm because her blood demanded it. Cultural and generational, and perhaps genetic, compulsions drove her desire.

Mom's dad, then more than sixty years old, had an acre of ground where he and Grandma, both Croatian immigrants from Zagreb, built a house, gardened on half the property and on the other half, nurtured apple, pear, cherry and black walnut trees in a mixed orchard. They also penned a calf, pig, or both at the back of the garden, and Grandpa fattened and butchered them. Then Grandpa smoked the meat in his backyard smokehouse.

Mom wanted to do the same, and more, on our twelve acres. Mom wanted to do twelve times as much on her twelve acres as Grandpa did on his one.

Dad did not share Mom's passion. He also was the child of immigrants, but his immigrant father, who grew up on a farm in Poland, came to this country to forget the sugar beet fields and demanding labor of the old country. He had owned a tavern in America, and my dad grew up helping his father with the tavern. So like his dad, my dad was a businessman – he would not toil on a farm. He would have been a tavern owner, too, but Mom wouldn't have it. So when Dad married Mom, he bought the hardware store, which turned out to be a blessing because it took him from the tavern's late nights and fights.

Dad would have preferred to stay in town, near his hardware store, but Mom begged him to buy the farm. He bought it, and as far as she knew, she got her way.

And being a pious woman, a matriarch who aimed at sainthood, she gave the twelve acres over to God.

Before we moved into the wood-frame house with the wrap-around porch, before my three sisters wiped the dust off the windowsills, before my older brother pulled one strip of yellowed wallpaper off the kitchen walls, before my dad paid to have the barn doors re-hung, before I sanded the pump handle on the well in the back yard, before my younger brother got in everyone's way, Mom painted a sign to fit under the peak of one end of the barn.

The plywood sign boasted heavy black lettering and a thick black border on its white background. Mom told my older brother, Bobby, to climb a ladder and pull down the judge's sign that had dubbed his acreage "Easy Acres."

Bobby replaced "Easy Acres" with Mom's sign, proclaiming the twelve acres "God's Acres." It was clearly visible from King Hill Road, which ran in front of the farmhouse.

When Bobby came down the ladder, we gathered in the barnyard, and Mom led us in an Our Father, a Hail Mary and a Glory Be.

Mom experienced her happiest moments when she was busy with more than she could accomplish in a lifetime. So she had children to help out, which was God's plan for men and women – have children and teach them to work.

First, there was Bobby, a few months from high school graduation; then Clara, two years behind him at sixteen; Terry, thirteen; Janice, eight; me, Bud, six; and Mark, four.

Dad wanted to wait a couple of months before moving so that we could have some work done in the farmhouse. The house only had two bedrooms.

But that didn't matter to Mom. She wanted in right away. She wanted in before St. Patrick's Day so that we could plant potatoes on the Irish patron saint's holy day. She borrowed a truck from one of her brothers, and Bobby, Clara and Terry moved the furniture.

Dad paid Mr. Williams, an old farmer who lived nearby on a small farm with a tractor to match, to plow the garden. The half-acre garden had not been tended for years – at least the four or five years the judge had owned the property.

Mom's dad, Grandpa Stjepan, came to help even though he had his own garden to tend. He took on more than he should, as Mom did, and he accomplished more in a day than three normal people could in the same twenty-four hours.

Grandpa couldn't sit still, and he didn't like cars. He walked the two miles to our farm, stopping at the grocery a quarter mile north of us to buy seven milk chocolate candy bars. He liked chocolate, something he didn't have growing up in Zagreb, so one of the candy bars was for him. The other six were for us. He brought seven every time he visited us. But when he came, we knew that we wouldn't see the chocolate until we were done with the work he came to help us with.

The girls started in the house, removing the dust of years of neglect by the widowed judge and the smoke from his pipe off the walls, ceiling, and floors. The girls cleaned the cobwebs out of the bare, rough attic, where Bobby, Clara, and Terry would sleep. A little later, Dad hired a contractor to renovate the attic into bedrooms. In the meantime, for privacy, Mom nailed a sheet across the attic to divide Bobby's bed from the two older girls' bed.

While the girls worked indoors, Bobby, Mark, and I went outside to the garden.

With shovel and wheelbarrow, Bobby cleaned out the chicken coop.

Mom was preparing to order chicks to raise for meat and eggs. We would slaughter all but a dozen layers once they reached butchering size. But first Bobby had to remove the chicken manure that had built up so high from chickens cared for by the previous owners that a male teen of a little less than average height had to bend over to avoid hitting his head on the coop's doorway.

Bobby shoveled the dried, caked manure into the wheelbarrow and carted it to the garden, where Grandpa Stjepan turned it into the soil with pitchfork and rake.

Mark and I were there, but we weren't much help. We squatted on our haunches and watched for earthworms near where Grandpa turned the soil. We heard people fished the deep holes of Contrary Creek, so we collected bait in case an opportunity arose to take our cane poles to one of the fishing spots.

Grandpa didn't talk much anytime, and he talked even less while he worked. He seldom stopped to rest once he started working, and once he started working, he didn't want anyone to get in his way. So while we watched and reached for worms, we had to take care that Grandpa didn't spear one of our hands with pitchfork or rake.

Bobby liked to talk. However, he wasn't in the mood for saying much that was positive. Every time he brought a load of manure to the garden, he complained about the cramped quarters in the chicken coop, the musty smell, the hard-packed manure, and the dust he raised as he plopped the dried and decayed poop into the wheelbarrow. He said he knew for sure that he would get some sort of lung fungus that would kill him. He said then Mom would be sorry.

Bobby may as well have been talking to the manure for all the sympathy he got from Grandpa.

We had half a can of worms and Bobby delivered about ten wheelbarrows of manure before Grandpa tired of Bobby's complaining and said something.

He said to Bobby, "Do you know what the white spot is on the chicken poop?"

"No, what is it?"

"It is the chicken poop, too."

I laughed. Mark found it funny, too. But Bobby wasn't in the mood for humor.

"That's stupid," Bobby said. "Is that an old country joke or some stupid farm joke you heard here?"

"You do not think it is funny?"

"No, I don't think it's funny."

Bobby spit.

"And I'm sick of this chickenshit," Bobby added.

Bobby looked to see if he made an impression on Grandpa. Grandpa Stjepan acted as if he hadn't heard Bobby, and disappointed, Bobby moved away, grumbling as he grudgingly shoved his wheelbarrow.

After Bobby was out of earshot, Grandpa said, "Bud and Mark, you do not say that word."

In the afternoon, Mom and the girls joined us outside to plant potatoes.

Grandpa sat on an upended bucket with a twenty-five pound bag of seed potatoes at his feet. He cut the seed potatoes into pieces, each piece with one or two eyes. Bobby, using a hoe, chopped grooves next to strings that Mom stretched from one end of the garden to the other. A perfectionist, Mom would not stand for rambling rows. She also demanded the cut pieces of potatoes be laid in the furrows a particular way.

"You have to plant them with the eyes up," Mom said.

Mom said eyes turned downward wouldn't send shoots up and out of the soil. That meant, of course, we couldn't drop the pieces in the furrows. We had to bend over and place each one in the ground.

We started working, and Clara whispered, "They will too turn and grow upwards. We learned that in school."

Soon Clara started dropping potato pieces when Mom wasn't watching.

Our mother wasn't easily deceived, though. Besides planting twice as many potatoes as any of us, she kept an eye on our rows. She caught Clara dropping, not positioning potatoes. Mom reproved Clara, who offered a religious argument in her defense.

"If it was true only eyes on top of the potato grow, why would God put eyes on the whole potato, even the bottom?" Clara said.

"The problem with smart people is all they do is talk and think about how they can get out of work, instead of work," Mom said.

That was pure Mom.

Mom appreciated learning, and she wanted us to be schooled. But at heart she was a workaholic. When it came to choosing between learning and physical labor, Mom would side with labor any day.

So we submitted to Mom's superstition, old wives' tale, or whatever it could be called, and we pressed the cut sides of the potatoes down into the soft soil, the eyes gazing toward heaven.

As we laid the last piece of potato to rest, Clara knelt by Grandpa, who pulled the candy bars from a pocket in his overalls.

"They can be planted eyes down and still grow up, can't they?" Clara said.

Grandpa handed Clara a candy bar.

He said, "Always with the eyes up."

St. Patrick's Day had been sunny and seasonable. But the weather deteriorated after that. Our seed potatoes, onion sets, and the seeds we planted – radishes, carrots, beets, lettuce, and peas – lay dormant in the cold ground.

March ended with the United States sending Explorer III into orbit. Sister Mary Andrew, my first-grade teacher at St. James Parochial School, read the newspaper story about the satellite to us. The satellite made it into orbit. It worked, but tumbled, and engineers couldn't stop the tumbling.

April brought better weather.

Fidel Castro and his rebel army attacked Havana.

Easter fell on April sixth. By then, days of growing sunshine helped green shoots emerge, cracking our garden's soil and unfolding wispy leaves searching for light and life.

We did the whole Easter observance at church, as always, beginning with Last Supper on Maundy Thursday. We spent most of Good Friday afternoon in church reciting the Litany of the Saints and the Way of the Cross, and marching in procession up and down the aisles of St. James Catholic Church. Holy Saturday, Monsignor O'Brien lit the Easter candle. Easter Sunday, Mark and I, dressed in crisp new suits and clip ties, wriggled and pulled at our clothes while Dad and Bobby enjoyed the comfort of their broken-in suits they got the year before. Clara, Terry and Janice wore smart new dresses that Mom had sewn. She made new dresses every Easter. That year, they were bright yellow dresses with white lace around the collar, hem and cuffs.

We lasted out the High Mass, then went home and changed. Mom fixed a picnic lunch, and the eight of us marched through the back half of our twelve acres. Mr. Halsel had planted the back six acres in wheat last fall. Mr. Halsel owned several hundred acres west of us over the hills and in the Missouri River Valley, and he went halves on acreage owned by rural dwellers, like my dad, who didn't have farm equipment and who worked in town.

We tramped through the wet field, laughing at our muddy shoes. Mark and I, carrying our cane fishing poles and can of worms, ran ahead of everyone. We stopped every now and then to wait for the others and throw dirt clods at the sky.

The girls, like little mothers, called to us not to get too far ahead.

We stayed in the lead only until we reached Contrary Creek. Mark and I then waited at the sharp edge of the field where it dropped immediately ten to fifteen feet to the creek. Bobby found a narrow path down a cross gully and through brush and trees, as well as the trash that someone had dumped to stop the rapid erosion, which led to the creek bed, a muddy mess of a ditch. But no one complained. We crossed a narrow place, walking on rocks and old tires sticking out of the water, to a low, dirt bank with spotty grass and sprouting weeds and wild sunflowers. We spread a blanket and ate.

Then Mark and I fished, catching the same perch over and over from a hole about three feet deep filled with murky water. Janice found a patch of clay in the embankment and pounded handfuls of the soil into plates, bowls, and cups. Terry didn't like to get her hands dirty, but without much else to do, she played in the clay, too.

Bobby and Clara rattled on and on about the St. Joseph high schools they attended. Bobby went to Christian Brothers, the Catholic school for boys, and Clara to the Convent of the Sacred Heart, the Catholic school for girls. Bobby would graduate in a couple of months. Bobby said that after graduation, he and his buddies – Bernie, Bean and Sonny – all would attend Missouri Western Junior College in downtown St. Joseph. City graduates received free tuition at the two-year school.

Mom talked about the farm and how we were all going to work to make it a good farm, a happy place, a prosperous and bountiful home.

Dad watched and smoked and smiled.

We were not in any hurry. It was a day with no place to be except there, in the bed of a creek named Contrary.

The sun eventually dropped behind the western hills. The air turned cool, too cool to remain in the creek, so we gathered our things and climbed the bank to our property. On the way, Bobby found a long vine that anchored itself in the top of a huge sycamore tree. Bobby had brought a hoe in case we needed to chop brush and weeds, and Bobby cut the root end of the vine. Then he swung out over the narrow stream on the loose end. Bobby and vine paused and drifted back to the bank. One by one, Clara, Terry, Janice and I took our turns. Mom said Mark couldn't swing on the vine, and he cried until Clara picked him up, swung him onto her back and told him to hang on.

"Clara, don't," Mom called, but she called too late to stop impetuous Clara, who propelled herself and Mark off the bank.

"Don't drop him," Mom called.

"I won't drop him," Clara called back with her usual confident air. "He has to hold on himself. I'm holding onto the vine."

Out she swung, farther than anyone else had arced over the creek. She was the family daredevil. There wasn't anything she wouldn't try and nothing that would get in her way.

Mark screamed like a banshee. That was Mark. He wanted to do everything until he was doing it. Then he screamed with fright and fear.

Dad and Bobby laughed. Janice and I jumped up and down, hollering about having another turn on the vine. Mom and Terry screamed at Mark to hold on.

Even with all the shouting, every one of us heard the tree branch holding the vine snap as a sharp crack of lightning snapped. Clara and Mark hung in mid-air, continuing their arc while the branch and vine were dropping, and we scattered to get out of the way of the crash.

No one remembered seeing Clara and Mark fall into the shallow water. But after racing like madmen to get away from the falling branches and vine, we raced back to the bank after the limbs and leaves settled. Clara and Mark were in the muck. Clara was waist deep in it, cackling as if she had just been on the greatest roller-coaster ride of her life. She pulled Mark, who had gone into the creek head first, out of the mire. Once out, he spit and coughed chocolate mud, and he cried in between the hacking and wheezing.

"You're all right. You're all right. That was fun," Clara said to Mark.

Mom waded out to Mark, losing her house shoes in the mud. Mom wiped Mark's face with Dad's handkerchief.

"He's just scared," Dad said.

"You shouldn't have done that, young lady," Mom said. "I knew something like that would happen."

Halfway home Mark finally cried the mud out of his eyes, nose and mouth. He stopped wailing.

"That was fun. Can we do it again?" he said.

"We had a good time, didn't we?" Mom said. "I'm so happy."

Introit Two

What is man?

Man is a creature composed of body and soul, and made in the image and likeness of God.

My mother was a doer. Even in the later stages of her illness, she opposed doing nothing. She kept her hands busy, mindlessly gripping, twisting, pulling and wringing the tail end of her blouse, a handkerchief, or the corner of the sheet on the bed on which she lay.

During her years as a mother and wife, she was never still.

When she finished the cooking, dishes, wash or housecleaning, she crocheted or embroidered, decorating pillowcases, dish towels and tablecloths. While Dad, my brothers and sisters and I stared at a television, she sat on the couch and created masterpieces of birds and flowers from bundles of colored thread that she stitched on stark white linen stretched across a small wooden, embroidery hoop.

Or she would do mundane needlework, hemming dresses and skirts, patching the knees of jeans, and darning the toes and heels of socks.

Though age slowed her mind in her last days, her hands were not ready to stop.

Her hands longed to patch socks with holes in toes and jeans with the knees ripped out or decorate with bundles of brightly colored thread squares of bold white linen.

Chapter Two

THE SUNDAY AFTER EASTER, Monsignor arrived to bless our farm.

He came with stole, holy water and aspergillum, a little hollow metal ball with holes that is stuck on a handle. Priests use the aspergillum to sprinkle holy water wherever holy water needs sprinkling.

Monsignor came from something-shire, Ireland. He was a stern man with a deep, controlled voice and a hard, solemn face. The movie "The Ten Commandments" came out two years before we moved to the farm. We were still familiar with the movie, and the uncanny similarity of Monsignor's voice to God's movie voice filled St. James elementary schoolchildren with awe and fear.

Terry, Janice and I were three of those children. When Dad drove to work, he took us with him to his hardware store, and we walked eight more blocks to the parochial school. Bobby and Clara drove the whole way to high school. Bobby drove Clara to the Convent; then he drove himself to Christian Brothers. The two schools were at the opposite end of town from our home.

Mom never considered sending us to public schools. That was not an option. She was Catholic through and through, and that meant religious instruction, nuns and Monsignor for us.

Once a week, Monsignor walked the halls of St. James School, entering each classroom to put fear in children.

"Who is God?" Monsignor boomed.

"God is the Supreme Being, infinitely perfect, who made all things and keeps them in existence," we replied.

"Why did God make us?"

"God made us to show forth His goodness and to share with us His everlasting happiness in heaven," we answered.

Then he carried his stern questions to the next classroom that accepted them with as much trepidation as the last classroom.

Monsignor brought his theocratic severity with him to bless our house. But he was human, too, or at least he tried to show a human side occasionally. After we stood in the living room with heads bowed and Monsignor sprinkled us and the room with holy water and consecrated words, the priest sat down to dinner in our dining room.

Monsignor's favorite diversion was teasing young boys by calling them Pat and Mike, two imaginary characters made famous in Irish jokes. Pat and Mike bungled their way through hundreds of anecdotes, not known for brevity, but protracted situational absurdity.

Monsignor called Mark and me Pat and Mike with his usual aplomb, leading into a patent Pat and Mike joke.

Pat and Mike were flying to America, and the four-engine plane lost one engine. The pilot said the plane would be half an hour late. Later the plane lost another engine, and the pilot said the plane would be an hour late. Then the plane lost a third engine, and the pilot said the plane would be two hours late.

Pat turned to Mike and said he hoped the fourth engine didn't quit or the plane would be up there all night.

We laughed, except for Mom. She didn't appreciate jokes. She thought jokes were juvenile and frivolous.

She often said, when we were joking during a meal, that we were too silly.

"Why can't you ever be serious?" she would say.

She didn't say that to Monsignor. Instead, she asked him if he had heard from his family. Everyone in church knew the story of Monsignor's family. His two brothers were parish priests, one in Cleveland and the other in the Chicago area. Monsignor also had seven sisters. Five of them were nuns in America. Three were teachers in parochial schools, the other two nurses in Catholic hospitals.

His parents had died. The two sisters without religious vocations remained in Ireland. They married and gave birth to several children.

Monsignor went back each year to visit them, and when he went, just about every adult male in St. James parish, including my father, gave the priest money to purchase Irish Sweepstakes tickets. No one at St. James won, but they purchased them as religiously as they went to church.

Monsignor said he stopped to visit his brother in Cleveland on the way back from Ireland. He said he didn't like Cleveland. Mom said she had never been to Cleveland.

She was not a traveled person. She had been several times to Kansas City, Kansas, sixty miles south, to visit second cousins and more distant relatives. Once, our family traveled to a small lake in northern Minnesota, where one of Dad's old Navy buddies operated a fishing resort, a dilapidated set of cabins in the middle of mosquito heaven. I was only about a year old when we went, so I didn't remember the trip, but the story in my family went that when Mom got back home, she told Dad, "I don't want to go on a trip there ever again. Next time we go on vacation, I want to go to New York and see a Broadway play."

Dad didn't care about plays, so we hadn't gone on a road trip since then. We spent a week in a cabin each summer at Bean Lake, an oxbow in the valley of the Missouri River thirty miles south of St. Joe.

We talked a little more about Monsignor's trip to Cleveland and his family. Mom focused on Monsignor's family and its affinity to religious vocations.

She said to Monsignor, "You should be proud of your family. My mother wanted me and my sisters to be nuns. But none of us are."

Monsignor said that being a mother was just as important as belonging to a religious order.

Mom believed that most of the time, but quite often, when she became upset with us, she would say, "Why didn't I listen to my mother and become a nun?"

Monsignor told Mom that perhaps, one of her children would be a priest or a nun, but he said the greatest good she could do for God was to be a good example to her children as the Blessed Mother was to her son. That's the way the meal ended, with Monsignor saying my mother should be like the Blessed Mother.

Mom and the girls went into the kitchen to do the dishes. Bobby went to the basement for a bottle of elderberry wine that Dad's dad made last summer. Dad and Monsignor went to the living room, where Bobby brought them each a glass of wine. Then Bobby disappeared, leaving Monsignor sitting in the easy chair and Dad on the divan. The living room filled with smoke from Dad's Camels and Monsignor's Lucky Strikes.

Mark and I played on the floor in the dining room, which led into the living room. We played with Lincoln Logs and Tinkertoys. The wooden logs, sticks and spindles clattered and clicked as we played, but I could hear the conversation between Dad and Monsignor.

They talked about the hardware business for a while. Then Monsignor talked about growing up under strict discipline and hard work, just as Mom did at her parents' one-acre workhouse. He concluded our farm would provide us children character.

"They don't need a farm for character," Dad said. "Their mother will lecture, pray, and boss it into them no matter what house they grow up in."

Monsignor laughed with deep, short huffs, more like coughs than chuckles.

"I had a mother like that," Monsignor said.

"I haven't told her, but these children probably won't spend much of their childhood here."

"Oh, no?" Monsignor said.

"The state is going to build a new road to DeKalb. They aren't going to replace the one out front of the house. They're going to pave one through the middle of this valley. It'll cut this farm in half."

"You'll still have both halves," Monsignor said.

"A new road brings development," Dad said.

"I see," Monsignor said.

I didn't see.

"Can I have some of your logs?" Mark asked me.

I had started making a cabin. I stopped while listening to Dad and Monsignor. Mark looked at me impatiently. I shoved my half-made cabin toward Mark and waited to hear more from Dad.

"J.R. is going to build homes on the west half after the road comes through," Dad said. "Twelve of them on half-acre lots."

I knew J.R. He was going to remodel our attic. He was going to convert it into two bedrooms, one for Bobby and another for Clara and Terry, starting next week.

"Hey, Bud."

Terry was calling from the kitchen.

"Bud, garbage."

"In a minute," I said.

"Now. Mom said."

"I'm coming," I said, but I lingered a moment hoping to hear more of Dad's conversation.

"Bud," Terry yelled. She was in the doorway and looking back at Mom. "He's still on the floor."

"Bud," Mom called from the kitchen. "Get moving."

I moved. I heard no more of Dad and Monsignor's conversation.

"When you're told to do something, you do it," Mom said.

"But Mom, listen. Dad and Monsignor were talking …"

"Yes, they were talking, and you're supposed to be minding your own business," Mom said. "Now take out the trash."

None of us ever pushed Mom very far. If we did, down to the basement we went, carrying a chair and Mom carrying her heavy plastic flyswatter with the big daisy on it. Mom knocked off most of the daisy's petals whacking our bare butts with it. She swatted flies with reckless abandon, and she swatted our disobedient bottoms with righteous abandon.

So out the door I went with the trash and garbage.

Taking out the garbage and trash were my jobs. We had a trash barrel by the back fence, about a hundred feet behind the house. The barrel was down a slight slope and after a line of four maple trees parallel to the back fence. Only a few feet separated the fence from the chicken coop on the opposite side, and the barn stood another fifty feet away.

First, I carried the trash to the barrel and dropped it in. Then I took the garbage to the edge of the garden where Mom set up a compost pile.

I was not an exceptionally brave child. I jumped at every pop, crack and chirp in the night, so I usually didn't stay outside very long. But I stayed out a little longer that night.

I was not an exceptionally astute child, either. Usually, I blabbered whatever I knew or heard. I could not keep a secret.

But something mysterious spoke to me that night. I paused at the edge of the garden and stared at the big sky, the quarter moon resting just above the hills of the eastern horizon, and the three apple trees glimmering in lunar light on the opposite side of the garden.

Something, maybe a glimmer of maturity, maybe the determined look on my mother's face telling me to take out the garbage, or maybe the disappointed face of my mother at times past when one of her children let her down told me that I shouldn't say anything about Dad's conversation with Monsignor.

I went back in the house with an empty pan. I handed it to Terry.

"What took you so long?" she said.

I didn't say anything. I didn't want to say anything. I was afraid to say anything so soon after making a resolution not to speak so much. I was afraid of what I might say.

Mom looked at me standing there speechless. I was afraid Mom could read my face even as I fought to keep my thoughts from showing on it.

"You have something on your mind?" Mom said.

"No," I said.

"Then go get ready for bed," she said.

I did, along with Janice and Mark. By the time we were ready for bed, Monsignor had left, and Janice, Mark and I climbed into the bed we shared.

Mark ground his teeth. Janice talked in her sleep. I listened to them a while. I thought about bulldozers leveling a road through our farm and what Mom was going to say to Dad when the heavy equipment cut our farm in half.

But the next day came, and the next, and the bulldozers had not arrived.

The next week came, and the wheat stood taller in the six-acre field. Mark and I ran through it trying to keep up with the wind that rippled the lengthening stalks and developing heads. But no road crossed our path.

Mom got her one hundred baby chicks. We kept them in the basement where their smell wafted up the cellar steps until they were old enough to move outside. We moved them out to the coop along with a lamp trailing an extension cord that reached the receptacle on the back porch. Mom bought Rhode Island reds, and they grew rapidly until they sported combs and wattles, and still the road wasn't built.

The Shah of Iran divorced his wife because she couldn't have children, a military coup led to a change of leadership in Algiers, and the Russians put another satellite, Sputnik III, into space, and the road was not built.

I forgot about the new highway. Our property was intact, and Mom said it was time to cull the roosters out of her flock. We built a fire with dead wood and heated a big pot of water.

"Bobby will chop their heads off," Mom said. "Clara will dip them in the hot water, and we'll pluck them. Bobby will gut them."

"How come I have two jobs?" Bobby said.

"It doesn't take long to chop off their heads or gut them," Mom said. "You can help pluck in between chopping and gutting."

"Why don't all of you just leave and let me do it all?" Bobby sassed.

"That can be arranged," Mom said.

Bobby knew Mom didn't mean it, and so did we. It was empty banter between a parent and an irritable teenager. So her warning was no threat, and my sisters and I didn't receive even momentary optimism from it. We would be there till the job was done.

Mom's plan sounded simple. It started simply awful.

Bobby chopped off the heads of about ten chickens, one after another. Headless poultry fluttered violently around the pen. We weren't prepared for that. Shocked, we stood as immovable as the wood block that Bobby laid the chickens' necks across before he whacked them with the ax.

"Get in here and grab a chicken," Mom yelled as she dashed about the pen after the stump-necked, blood-spurting chickens.

We edged into the pen as if we were entering a house of horror. None of us could say afterward why Mark went in ahead of us, but he was at the front. A sudden panic attack overcame him, and he was screaming, running, and flailing, not out of the pen, but into the chicken melee. One headless chicken attacked him, and Mark bolted into the chicken wire fence. He clung to it, calling for someone to deliver him from the demon-inspired chicken that flapped at his legs and fluttered up his back squirting a ragged path of blood across the back of his T-shirt.

The chicken finally collapsed, but Mark continued to scream and weep. Terry rescued him. She kicked the dead chicken away, took Mark into her arms, and whisked him into the house.

"Come on," Mom said. "Let's go to work."

We went to work without Terry or Mark. Mark didn't matter, but we all grew angry at Terry who didn't pluck one stinking feather that day.

Introit Three

Hail Mary, full of grace, the Lord is with thee. Blessed art thou among women, and blessed is the fruit of thy womb, Jesus. Holy Mary, mother of God, pray for us sinners now and at the hour of our death. Amen.

Several years ago, we had a summer reunion at a lake in northwest Arkansas, where Terry lived. Janice brought Mom. She could still get around. She looked fine, but she repeated questions, and she didn't know any of her grandchildren.

She had forgotten me. She called me Mark. She remembered her other children by name, but not me. I didn't take it personally.

"Do you remember, Mark, how you fell in the creek with Clara? I thought you drowned in the mud," she said.

Then a look of horror came over her face, and a flood of anguish formed in the corners of her eyes. I laid my hand on her shoulder. She touched the cuff of her blouse to her eyes.

"It's okay. Clara pulled me out of the mud. Do you remember?"

She nodded. I moved away, and I avoided her the rest of the reunion.

Chapter Three

PLUCKING AND GUTTING DECAPITATED chickens turned out to be about the worst job in the world. The smell of hot, wet chicken feathers and intestinal tracts leaking green bile and half-digested cracked corn and grass made the job near intolerable.

Clara and Janice made good hands at any chore, but even they grew nauseous at the poultry stench.

Plucking chicken feathers proved the toughest and most tedious job of slaughtering any animal. Bobby and I plucked horridly. We left big feathers and small ones, and mostly pinfeathers, the little black tips of feathers barely sticking out of the chicken's skin. Mom or Clara had to clean up what we started. Finally, Mom told me to stop plucking. She told Bobby to slice open the chickens' bellies and let me gut them.

Except for the smell, I didn't mind reaching inside the warm cavities, which were about the right size for my hands. I pulled the organs out, and eventually, Mom let me use a knife to free the gizzards, hearts and livers, which I put into separate bowls.

But the headless chickens lying in the dirt of the chicken yard seemed to have no end. The morning of chickens turned into the afternoon of chickens. The afternoon of chickens turned into the evening of chickens. Mom determined that we were going to butcher all but a dozen hens, and when Mom made up her mind to do something, we all did it. Even when the task turned into more than she bargained for, she wouldn't give in.

Persistence is a good trait to have, but Mom had persistence to a fault. She wanted us to have it too. But she didn't teach persistence in short stages. We were supposed to learn it the way she learned it – all at once from hard parents and hard times.

"You know, we aren't in the Depression anymore," Bobby told Mom. "You can buy chicken for nineteen cents a pound, can't you?"

"That's nineteen cents we can save," Mom said.

"By time you figure the cost of the chicks, the eight you lost, the cost of feed, heating this water and freezing the meat, these chickens probably cost you more than nineteen cents a pound."

Mom didn't answer.

"We could spend our time doing other things," Bobby said.

"Like what?" Mom said.

"Reading, creative things, music."

Bobby enjoyed reading and music. Whatever money he earned, he spent on LP albums and books. He was into Russian novels lately. He was reading Dostoevsky, and he wanted to get a copy of Boris Pasternak's "Dr. Zhivago," which came out that year.

Mom gave him a look of total incomprehension and a shake of her head. Mom believed you read the newspaper in the morning, and in the evening when you finished your work, you could pick up a book.

"When we get done with these chickens, you can read all you want."

"That's the thing, though," Bobby said. "There'll only be something else when we're done with this."

Bobby was right. Mom never noticed our flagging energy, our dwindling conversation, our increasing sighs and moans. If she did, she ignored them.

"Work is never done. You'll find that out when you get a job," Mom said.

Bobby mumbled, "Any job has to be better than this."

He would soon find out about jobs.

Bobby graduated from high school less than a month before. The graduates of Christian Brothers and the Convent of the Sacred Heart – who never saw each other in their school halls except for occasional dances and pep rallies

– met in St. Joe's downtown cathedral to receive their diplomas. Bishop John Cody, head of the Diocese of Kansas City-St. Joseph, gave the graduation speech. A huge man with a voice as deep as the nave of the structure, Bishop Cody commanded awe. If the pope was God to us, Bishop Cody was Michael the Archangel.

We were elated at Bobby's graduation because Bobby was the first in our family to graduate from high school. Dad finished tenth grade before going to work full time at his dad's tavern. Mom went to work after her eighth year of school. She picked strawberries in the spring and tomatoes in the summer in local fields. She made ten cents an hour before she was old enough to work at one of the packing houses in south St. Joe.

She stripped cattle intestines, squeezing them to flush out the green and brown waste then rinsing them with water that puddled messily at her feet. The intestines came to her in barrels, and when the barrels were about two-thirds empty, that was the extent of her flat-footed reach. Then she had to lean over, nearly falling into the barrels, to pull out the last strings of guts.

Only marriage and children freed her from the bowels of the packing house.

And even more than twenty-five years later, the greatest opportunity for work for young people in St. Joseph remained the packing houses.

Mom and Dad expected all of us children, once out of high school, but still at home, to work so that we could pay room and board even if we continued our education at college.

There was no escape from work for Bobby, only an escape from work on the farm, so he begged one of Mom's brothers who worked at one of the packing houses for a job. Uncle Stephen got Bobby one, one that didn't last long, barely a week. Bobby didn't work inside the packing house, but outside lining up cattle traveling the chute that led from the stockyards, over the main roadway, and into the killing room. The doomed cattle followed the Judas cow, a cow who took the walk only to be turned away from the entrance to the packing house in order to take the lead again for the next bunch of condemned cattle.

Mom taught us to be conscientious workers, but Bobby, maybe because it was his first job, got a little sloppy. He said afterwards that a steer in the middle of the line turned and jammed the chute. He said he walked back to help another worker get the turned steer pointed in the right direction.

When he did, the Judas cow, for some reason, became confused and marched into the packing house. Unfortunately for Bobby, the packinghouse killing room had a fresh hand who wasn't familiar with the Judas cow even though it wore a bell.

The Judas cow took the mechanized hammer in the forehead. She went down, then up on the hook for processing. Workers on the line immediately recognized the Judas cow, an animal they loved as a pet. She'd been doing her job faithfully for more than five years. Some of the workers brought her special feed rations, and at the summer company picnics, the Judas cow gave the workers' children rides on her back.

Most of the workers were devastated. Some were so distraught that they went home for the day. Bobby and the new worker in the killing room went home for good. Mom's brother said he would never again arrange a job for any of his nephews, which led to some ill feelings toward Bobby from cousins.

While Bobby waited for a call after putting in a dozen applications at retail stores and restaurants, he found plenty of work on the farm, just as he feared. Green beans and lima beans were maturing. Beets and carrots needed pulling, washing, and set in sand in the root cellar. Tomatoes ripened, and about half a bushel of them were ready to pick any day of the week. Cornstalks grew fuzzy tassels, their ears filled, and they needed shucking before Mom dropped them in boiling water, sliced off the kernels and froze or canned them.

Mom processed everything, and the shelves lining the basement slowly filled with rows of canned green beans and lima beans; peas; tomatoes, tomato sauce and tomato juice; corn; pickled beets; sweet, dill, and bread-and-butter pickles; pears; and apple jelly, applesauce, and apple butter. And in between vegetable picking, washing, snapping, chopping and cutting, the garden needed hoeing, the yard and fence line mowing, and the barn painting, cleaning, and repairing.

The barn was one of those old, solid barns that could last forever if the roof shed water, but it had been neglected and the roof leaked. If Mom was going to get a milk cow and other animals, the barn needed help. Bobby had to give it the help it needed.

Dad didn't want any animals, especially a milk cow, but we ended up with one. A farmer with a dairy came into Dad's hardware store and made Dad a deal. The dairyman had a cow about a month from calving and he wanted to sell her. Mom happened to be in the store, and she talked Dad into buying the cow. She was a Guernsey, and we found out why the farmer didn't want her. The cow, psychologically, was a mess. She suffered from depression, anxiety and a host of phobias. Few of us could get near her. We named her Krazy Kow.

We wondered who would be able to milk her because even when we blinked, she flinched, jumped, and glared suspiciously.

Mom and Dad feared what she might do to one of us younger children, so it was left up to Bobby and Clara to feed Krazy Kow. Clara seemed to find something appealing in the cow's psychoses and obstinacy, but Bobby hated the animal. If Clara made any gains winning Krazy Kow over, Bobby negated them by screaming and throwing things.

The summer turned into the season of discontent for Bobby.

But for Janice, Mark and me, the summer offered a time of adventure, running through the pasture and fields, exploring the ditch and Contrary Creek, though Mom didn't like us down there. We worked, but we also had time to play because Mom didn't want us in the kitchen when she was canning. If we could have helped, we would have been there, and we did some preparing, but when hot water and steam were involved, she released us from the kitchen.

One mid-summer day, she was canning, we were playing, and Mom sent Bobby, Clara and Terry out to chop weeds between the road in front of the house and the pasture fence. Mom wouldn't stand for overgrown fence lines.

The older children whacked the weeds with whips, handles about three feet long with flat, serrated blades turned on edge. They swung the whips as if they were golf clubs, and Bobby, Clara and Terry left plenty of space between each other as they hacked away.

Grandpa Stjepan had just left after sitting down a few minutes with Janice, Mark and me in the front yard. We sat on a blanket spread across the grass warmed by a July sun. Mom gave us crackers and Kool-aid, and we had Hershey chocolate bars that Grandpa left with us and Janice's play tea set. We were lost in make-believe. Janice served in Victorian style and bonnet, while I drank and ate with Wild West abandon and play revolvers strapped to my hips. Mark saw no discrepancy between the two.

Up the road to the north, my older brother and two oldest sisters chopped, complained, cursed and wished they were anywhere else in the world. Bobby had just walked away from Clara and Terry after a break, when a passing car stopped. A young man got out and started talking to the two girls. I watched them, wondering who the young man was when Janice screamed. She jumped up and dashed toward the house. She had taken about five steps when she turned and came back to grab Mark's hand, pulling him off the blanket and toward the house. All the time her eyes were on the fence behind me.

"Move, Bud, run to the house," she screamed.

Down the road, the girls and boys heard Janice's cry. They ran toward us.

"Snake, Bud," Janice screamed while running with Mark. "Snake, snake."

I looked over my shoulder and saw a long, but thick, tan and brown snake wrapped around the horizontal bar of the fence.

Janice and Mark met Mom coming out of the house. Mom wielded a broom. Janice pointed to the fence, and Mom charged, swinging the broom into attack position. I had a ringside seat for the fight. I never moved. I had a bad habit of freezing in perilous situations. It was part of my nature. I didn't like it. But that's the way it was.

I sat there while Mom battered the snake that had no chance of escape. It was winding its way down the wire to make for the nearby gully when Mom smacked it over and over. It writhed on the ground, but Mom didn't know that the snake was dead, that nerves made it move even after it suffered injuries that rendered it lifeless. She didn't stop smacking until the teenagers arrived and the youth who stopped to talk to Clara and Terry told her the snake was dead.

"It's still moving," Mark said.

Janice and Mark edged up to see the mauled intruder.

"It's nerves," the young man said. "It's dead."

We stared at the youth. He reached a hand toward Mom.

"Hi, I'm Thomas Groom. I live two roads down."

Mom nodded, ignoring his hand, but Bobby shook it and introduced himself to Thomas.

"What kind of snake is it, Bobby?" Janice said. "Is it poisonous?"

Bobby shrugged his shoulders.

"It's a bull snake," Thomas said. "They're not poisonous, but they'll bite if you bother them."

"Well, it's nice to meet you. You can get back to cutting weeds, you three," Mom said, and she handed me the broom. "Bud, you throw it in the ditch."

Mom marched back into the house.

"The poor snake just showed up in the wrong place at the wrong time," Thomas said as we watched the snake's curling motion gradually slacken. "My mom doesn't like them either."

Mom hated snakes. We didn't know it until then, but she would never meet a snake that she could walk away from without hitting, thrashing or whacking, no matter how small or colorful they were. If Mom saw one, big or small, fast or slow, it was dead after a clobbering by broom, hoe, stick or rake — whatever was handy.

The bigger children headed back up the road. Clara and Terry obviously were taken with Thomas. Bobby didn't seem to hit it off right away with the young man. He was barely sixteen, and self-assured.

After they left, I used the handle end of the broom to lift the snake and carry it to the ditch. Janice tried to get a closer look, and trying to be funny, I poked the broom with the snake on the end at her. My sense of humor was never very good.

The snake slid off the broom and flopped into Janice's face. She ran screaming into the house. I knew I was in trouble. I gathered the snake as fast as I could and went to the ditch with it. Soon Mom was in the driveway calling for me.

Mark was there, too, telling her I threw the snake at Janice.

I told Mom it was an accident, but Mom said accidents don't happen unless someone is goofing around. She whisked me to the basement and gave me a beating with the daisy flyswatter.

That was the day Bobby got in more trouble than I got into, though.

Janice, Mark and I had just gone to bed when the phone rang. Dad answered it. After he hung up the phone, he and Mom carried on a discussion in low, serious voices. The only thing we could make out was that Dad said that he would pick up Clara and Terry, who were visiting girlfriends in town, and then go get Bobby.

"Clara can drive Bobby's car back home," Dad said.

We couldn't go back to sleep. Mom banged things in the kitchen. Never a quiet person, she was louder when angry, and her every movement ended with a clank or thump.

Clara and Terry came home first. Clara drove Bobby's car just as Dad said she would, and Mom told the two to get upstairs and to bed. If there was any phrase Mom said more often than "Get to work," it was "Get to bed."

Dad pulled into the drive with Bobby about a half hour later. They went into the living room and that's when the yelling started. Mom yelled the most, but Dad interrupted Mom several times. He didn't usually do that, so we knew it was serious.

They said things like "We thought you knew better than that," and "What were you thinking?" and "Do you know what sort of serious consequences this could have had?"

Mark slept through it all. Janice and I got out of bed and went into the kitchen. I sat at the table while she poured each of us a glass of milk. Then she sat down.

"I didn't mean to hit you with the snake," I said. "I was just fooling. I didn't know it was going to fly off the broom."

"Yes, you did," she said. "You did it on purpose."

There wasn't any use discussing it. I picked up a cookie from a plate of cookies that Janice brought over from the counter top.

"Do you like the farm?" I said.

"Sometimes," Janice said. "I miss my friends where we used to live. There's only you and Mark here. Don't you miss your friends?"

A few of my classmates at St. James lived up the street from where we used to live. I hadn't really missed them. I shrugged my shoulders. As I looked at the cookie I was eating, something about it struck me as interesting.

"I miss the store-bought cookies I used to eat at John's house up the street," I said. "All we ever eat are cookies Mom bakes."

Janice went back to bed. I climbed the steps. Clara and Terry had a room at the head of the stairs off to the north. A hallway led to Bobby's room at the front of the house. I looked in the girls' room, where Terry was in bed. She was praying. She worked a rosary with her fingers.

"What are you doing?"

"I'm praying for Bobby," Terry said.

She had the softest heart in the family, except for Mark, but he was just a child and didn't know better.

I walked into Bobby's room. The front window was open, and the screen was propped against the foot of his bed. I looked out and Clara was sitting on the porch roof with her back to me, wisps of smoke curling around her head. I climbed out and sat next to her. She was smoking. She handed her cigarette to me.

"Here, have a smoke."

I took it. I had never smoked. I didn't know until that day that Clara smoked. I choked as I puffed on the cigarette.

"Keep at it," Clara said getting another cigarette from her pocket and lighting it. "You'll get used to it."

She told me what happened. Bobby drove across the Missouri River Bridge to Wathena, Kansas, with his friends to go drinking. In Missouri, the drinking age was twenty-one, but in Kansas, it was eighteen. So Bobby and his friends had been drinking at a bar. They also ended up with a six-pack and brought it back to Missouri. They stopped along a county road and were drinking the beer when a deputy happened by. He didn't take Bobby or the other boys in. He knew their families and had the dispatcher call Dad to come get Bobby and his buddies. The officer gave them a warning and a break.

But Bobby wasn't getting a break from Mom and Dad. Clara and I could hear the muffled rebukes meant for Bobby coming from downstairs.

I told Clara thanks for telling me about Bobby, and I thanked her for the cigarette.

"If you ever need a cigarette, I have some," Clara said. "Just don't tell Mom."

"Okay," I said. Now I had two secrets.

That was the most excitement that summer until Krazy Kow had her calf.

Bobby ended up with a job washing dishes at a restaurant on our end, the south end, of town, and he stayed out of trouble between the job and the farm.

He even stopped tormenting Krazy Kow, and with Clara's patience, the cow quieted some. Clara was excited as Krazy Kow's time drew near and that's all she talked about. But she was away the night Krazy Kow's calf came, the night I helped pull her calf.

On a Friday, Dad came home from work and checked on Krazy Kow in the pasture. He found a tongue sticking out of the cow's back end.

Dad figured something was wrong and called Mr. Williams, the farmer who plowed our garden.

Dad, Mark and I went with Mr. Williams to the pasture and herded Krazy Kow into the barn. Dad disappeared, leaving us with Mr. Williams. The old farmer looked around.

"Where'd your dad go?" he asked.

"He does that," I said, which was true. Dad would get us started on a job, then disappear. It didn't seem abnormal to us, but Mr. Williams appeared put out.

"I need a cord and a rope," Mr. Williams said.

He bullied Krazy Kow into a stanchion, something we never had the experience or nerve to do, while I got a short piece of cord and a rope. He told me not to go away. He reached inside Krazy Kow's back end and poked around until he pulled out two front hooves. He tied the two hooves together with the cord; then he tied one end of the rope around the cord between the hobbled front hooves.

"Loop the other end around a board on that opposite stall," Mr. Williams said. "Make it taut."

Mr. Williams told me he was going to bounce on the rope and each time he came up, I was supposed to pull the slack out of the rope.

Mr. Williams started slowly bouncing on the rope by sitting on it and raising himself on his legs. A few bounces drew the front legs of the calf out to their knees. I tightened the rope.

Mr. Williams bounced some more and the snout of the calf appeared. I tightened the rope once more, and Mr. Williams bounced until the head and front shoulders appeared. Krazy Kow bawled so loudly that a passerby hearing the bawls would have thought the sounds were coming from an elephant, and every time Mr. Williams bounced, she arched her back and her entire body tensed.

Then with one big Krazy Kow push and Mr. Williams' last bounce, the calf came free as if Krazy Kow's orifice were a mouth spitting out a pumpkin seed. The calf hit the floor with a thud that made me cringe, but Mr. Williams said, "Don't worry. The calf's all right."

He untied the rope and cord from the calf, and he loosed Krazy Kow from the stanchion. Krazy Kow didn't pay any attention to her calf. She walked away from it.

She ended up by Mark. His eyes were as big as Krazy Kow's, and he stared at her in horror. Krazy Kow expelled the afterbirth at Mark's feet.

Mark's face blanched, and his chest heaved. Krazy Kow never gave a thought to cleaning up her calf, but she turned and began chewing on the afterbirth.

Mark's dry heaving became fruitful. He added vomit to the red mass on the barn floor.

"I guess that's the first birth he's seen," Mr. Williams said.

Introit Four

O God, Who in the humility of Thy Son hast raised up a fallen world; grant perpetual gladness unto Thy faithful people; that whom Thou hast rescued from the perils of endless death, Thou mayest cause to enjoy endless happiness. Through the same our Lord. Amen.

Bobby called me one night when Janice was caring for Mom. Bobby said he watched Mom so Janice and her husband could have a night out and see a movie.

Bobby said he read to Mom, who showed no signs of recognizing him or comprehending what he was reading. While Bobby was reading, Mom dirtied her diaper.

Bobby was going to change it, but Mom wouldn't let Bobby pull her gown up. She kept her legs locked tight.

Bobby said he had to ask a lady across the street to help. Mom let the neighbor lady change the diaper.

"Here's a woman who doesn't recognize anyone, can't remember what happened yesterday or the day before, yet her sense of modesty is so strong she wouldn't let a man change her messy diaper."

Chapter Four

DAD PUT THE BUCKET under Krazy Kow. The cow promptly kicked the bucket away. Dad cursed, put the bucket back. He sat down on the three-legged stool and reached for Krazy Kow's teats. Her back left hoof caught Dad on the back of his right hand before the bucket went flying across the barn.

Dad cursed again and went into the house, leaving Krazy Kow locked in the stanchion and us amused, but not laughing, at his misery and incompetence.

This was supposed to be Dad's big moment. For years, he told us about spending a month each summer when he was a youth with a farm family in Savannah, about twelve miles north of St. Joe.

None of us knew how much the death of Dad's mom – she died when he was seven – had to do with summers in Savannah, but those days on the dairy farm formed the foundation for some of his favorite stories. He said he knew how to milk cows. He was going to show us, but it didn't work out that way.

Mom shook her head, picked up the bucket that now had a dent in it, and sat down on the stool. The direct opposite of Dad, who leaned away from the recalcitrant cow and worked timidly, Mom leaned her head and left shoulder into Krazy Kow's flank and milked with confidence.

Mom steadied the bucket with one hand and grasped a teat with the other. Krazy Kow swiped at the bucket, but Mom was too quick for her. Mom moved the bucket and put it back in place, timing it perfectly to catch a squirt of milk she forced out of Krazy Kow's udder.

"Once she discovers how good it feels for her to be relieved of milk, she'll be more patient," Mom said.

Mom went from one teat to the next, always moving the bucket ahead of Krazy Kow's stomps. Krazy Kow gradually gave up, and Mom worked with two hands, getting half a bucket of milk.

Mom looked at us.

"Who's next?" she said.

Clara jumped on the stool and emptied Krazy Kow out so quickly that no one ever challenged her for the milking job afterward.

Terry tried it once. Clara stayed in town late one night after school for something, and Mom sent Terry out. But Terry came back in the house carrying a dry bucket. Tears streamed down her face. Krazy Kow didn't kick her, Terry said, but the cow had done everything to try.

Mom had to do the milking that time, and that's the way it was if Clara couldn't.

We gave the calf the first milk from Krazy Kow, then milk supplement for a week before Dad sold the calf. Mom wanted to keep it, but Dad was anxious to recover some of the money he spent on Krazy Kow.

Bobby complained that Krazy Kow, like the chickens and vegetables, was more expensive than the benefits she provided. But no one could argue that the delicious whole milk from Krazy Kow was not worth the cost of keeping her.

Then there was the cream. Mom threatened us with torture in the basement to keep us from drinking the cream once it cooled in the jar in the refrigerator. If the cream survived, we turned it into butter for the table and whipped cream for cakes and pies.

And even though Krazy Kow had a wacky temperament, she supplied us with much more milk than we needed or wanted. Mom took milk to her dad and mother, and Mom sold some to her brothers and sisters.

Besides Clara and Mom, one other person could milk Krazy Kow. It came as a surprise.

One night, Bobby invited his buddies over to play pitch. A gregarious, humorous young man, Bobby attracted many friends who stopped by the house often – except for lately when Bobby had been in the dumps over working at the farm and washing dishes at the restaurant. But with college days approaching, Bobby's good humor and amiability returned. His friends came around once again.

Bernie, Bean and Sonny stopped over one Friday, a night when Mom and Dad went to the church basement for a card party that raised money for the parochial school. They left, and the boys sat down at the kitchen table with a deck of cards. Mark and I sat down with them. They ignored us, but we could live with that as long as we could watch.

They played five-point pitch. That's what they always played – high, low, jick, jack, game. They put up money too, sometimes a nickel, dime or quarter per point.

Clara, Terry and Janice were on the swing on the front porch. They sat out there with Thomas. He began stopping by to visit Clara and Terry. Mom didn't like him for one very simple reason: He was Baptist.

If Mom could have seen past Thomas' religion, she would have seen another reason to dislike him. He was more interested in Terry than Clara. It was evident in the way his eyes smiled at Terry. Clara could see it, too, if she would admit it, but she wouldn't. Clara wouldn't admit what was evident.

She was all angles and sharp features.

Terry was gentle curves and soft skin.

Clara was loud, pushy at times. She challenged people with her nervous eyes and quick tongue.

Terry's eyes were calm. She laughed subtly, never harshly, and she complimented people. Clara found fault with people whom she didn't like and teased them roughly.

Thomas could tolerate Clara's coarseness, but he wasn't interested in her. Mom didn't suspect that. With old-fashioned, matrimonial customs in mind, Mom thought Thomas should be interested in her oldest daughter. Besides,

Clara was an obvious flirt.

So when Mom left with Dad, she told Bobby to keep an eye on Thomas. He was two months Clara's junior, but even younger looking because of his tow head and dimples. Mom said that when Thomas flashed his disarming smile, he almost could make her forget that he was a Baptist.

Bobby and his buddies played about an hour. They were a noisy bunch, talking and joking loudly with one another, slapping cards on the table, analyzing and arguing fiercely at the end of each game the sequence of the cards just played.

Somehow the conversation came around to the farm, the farm work, and the farm cow.

Bobby said Krazy Kow couldn't be milked by anyone except Clara. Always doubting the claims of others, Bernie said he never milked a cow before, but he thought he could do it.

"It can't be that hard," Bernie said. "You just get hold of their tits and squeeze like this. My dad showed me how one time."

He made a squeezing motion with his right hand.

"Your dad's never milked a cow," Sonny said.

Sonny lived next door to Bernie. They didn't agree on anything, but they were seldom apart.

"I'll bet you the money I have here on the table that you can't get a quart of milk out of her," Bobby said. "I'll bet you can't get a pint of milk out of her."

"How much you got?" Bernie said.

Bobby counted it out.

"Five thirty-five."

"You're on," Bernie said.

"I'm in," Sonny said. He had about ten dollars.

Bean jumped in on the bet. He said he had milked a cow before. Bobby reiterated his claim that not one of the three or the three as a unit could get a pint of milk out of the cantankerous cow.

Bobby went to the front door, calling Clara. She came in followed by Terry, Thomas and Janice.

Bobby told her to get Krazy Kow and put her in the stanchion.

"What for?" Clara said. "What do you want with her?"

"To settle a bet," Bobby said.

"What's it about?"

"It's nothing. Don't worry. We're not going to hurt her," Bobby said.

Clara wasn't convinced.

"I've already mil …" Clara started, but Bobby shushed her and waved to his buddies to follow him.

"Come on, we'll get Krazy Kow ourselves," he said, and they were out the door, running into the dark pasture with Clara's curses following them.

Out the door, Thomas, Terry, Janice, who pulled Mark by one hand, and I went too. We went to the barn and stood outside the fence while Krazy Kow rushed through the wide open barn door, the boys and Clara following. Then the older youths climbed over the fence and we smaller people went between the slats.

The boys locked Krazy Kow in the stanchion, and the clamor of screaming youths and children made Krazy Kow hyper and paranoiac. She yanked at the stanchion and stomped while we danced around each other and jumped.

"You better not hurt her," Clara screamed.

She ran to Thomas and shoved him, trying to get him to intervene.

"Stop them," Clara called to Thomas.

"They're just having a little fun," Thomas said. "They're more likely to get hurt than Krazy Kow is."

Clara shot Thomas a hateful look, one our family knew and feared. But Thomas didn't know better. He held her by an arm to keep her from charging Bobby and his friends as Bernie sat down on the stool with a fool's confidence.

Confidence, though, couldn't squeeze milk out of Krazy Kow, and Bernie couldn't get hold of her teats. She jerked at the stanchion and twisted her back end away from Bernie. With one quick swivel, Krazy Kow swung her hips and slapped Bernie off the stool and onto the dirt, straw and manure of the barn floor. Trying not to be intimidated by Krazy Kow or our uproarious laughter, Bernie jumped up and back onto the stool as he righted it, only to be knocked over again.

"It's my turn. Let me at her," Bean cried, rushing to Krazy Kow's side.

Bean stood over Bernie, who was checking to see if his arms and legs still moved.

"Okay, you guys, stop," Clara called.

But Bean was reaching under Krazy Kow and had hold of a teat while trying to move the bucket into position. Krazy Kow pulled against the stanchion, and with a mighty jerk, the wooden lock cracked and popped as if the eight-by-eight posts of the barn were collapsing and the roof was following it to the ground.

Krazy Kow's rear end hit the ground and she rolled over. Bernie and Bean jumped up and everybody, except me, scattered with screams and laughter. As usual, I froze as Krazy Kow righted herself. Carrying the separated stanchion around her neck, she backed straight for me.

I would have been trampled, but Thomas pulled off his T-shirt and draped it over Krazy Kow's head and put his arms around her neck, holding her tightly and digging his heels into the dirt floor. Once Thomas stopped Krazy Kow, Clara rushed to help him. She opened the stanchion so that it dropped off the cow's neck. Krazy Kow ended up with a cut behind her right ear. Otherwise, she was fine physically. Emotionally, she was a mess. For several mornings and evenings, Thomas came to help Clara milk Krazy Kow, and he had to do most of the milking.

The night of the bet, though, after Thomas and Clara had settled Krazy Kow down, Bobby, his friends, Terry and Janice with Mark went to the door of the barn and peeked in. When Clara saw the boys, she ran after them, screaming threats. They ran from her, laughing and taunting her. Before long we were all running after each other through the barnyard and the yard of the house. The game ended when Sonny knocked Mark down. Mark cried, but he was fine.

Terry was brushing Mark's clothes off and patting his back, when Bernie said, "I want another chance at milking that cow?"

We all groaned, but Thomas said, "Even if she'd stand still for you, you aren't about to get a pint of milk out of her. Clara milked her out only a couple hours ago."

Bernie, Bean and Sonny called Bobby a cheat. They picked him up and threw him in the water trough.

Summer drew to a close quickly after that. Arab nationalists murdered King Faisal in Iraq, overthrowing the monarchy. U.S. Marines landed in Beirut to protect the pro-Western government in Lebanon. Queen Elizabeth gave her son the title Prince of Wales, an American nuclear sub became the first vessel to cross the North Pole, and the United States put Explorer IV into orbit.

I wasn't ready to return to school, but the girls were, and Bobby was anxious to start college. A few days before we headed back to St. James Parochial School, Bobby and his buddies went to Missouri Western Junior College to register for fall classes. He left early in the morning and didn't come back when he should have.

That evening, Mom kept asking us if we knew where Bobby was. We didn't know anything except he hadn't come home. Clara had gotten a phone call from him in the afternoon, but she didn't tell anyone what Bobby said, and she went up to her room after talking to him.

Janice and I were in the kitchen when Bobby came home near bedtime. Janice and I each had a pint jar of cream that we shook, churning the white liquid into butter. We heard the front door open.

After we heard Bobby mumble something, Mom yelled "You did what?"

Mom, Dad and Bobby went into the living room. We couldn't hear everything. But we heard Mom crying and Dad saying, "Why didn't you talk this over with us?"

My pint jar of cream had turned into a lump of butter. I put the jar in the refrigerator and went up the stairs. Terry was in her room, kneeling by her bed, a rosary in her hands. I waved to her. Then I went to the open front window and climbed out on the porch roof.

Clara handed me a cigarette.

"What's going on?" I said.

"Bobby joined the Army," Clara said.

"I thought he was going to college."

"Nope, he changed his mind."

I waited. Clara told me what happened. Bobby signed up for twelve hours of college classes; then he went to settle his bill. Bobby was expecting a small bill. St. Joseph paid the tuition for city students who went to Mo West. But when Bobby gave his address, Rural Route 6, the clerk said he wasn't inside the city and didn't qualify for free tuition.

"Bobby said he told the lady he lived inside the city all his life except for the last six months, but she said he didn't qualify," Clara said. "He was going to have to come up with two hundred and fifty dollars for tuition."

"What's that have to do with the Army?" I said.

"Bobby said he was so mad about the tuition bill that he went down the street and enlisted in the Army. He catches a bus Friday for Texas."

Somebody visiting our house that week would have thought there was a death in the family. We didn't smile or laugh. We didn't talk. We moped through the house. On Friday, Bobby got his things together, and Mom made a sack lunch for him. Mark and I went with her as she drove Bobby to the bus station.

Mom asked him if he had his underwear, toothbrush, and papers. Bobby grunted, "Yes," each time. Several times, Mom acted as if she was going to say something, something that wasn't a question about mundane things, and you could see the words caught in her throat. She would swallow hard and tighten her grip on the steering wheel.

We got to the bus station early. Mom didn't believe in being late for anything, even unpleasant affairs. We sat in the lobby for a while, then Bobby said he had to go to the bathroom. I went with him.

We were standing by the urinals when he told me, "You're the big brother while I'm gone. You take care of your sisters."

I told Bobby that he didn't have to go – it wasn't too late to change his mind.

"You don't understand the Army," Bobby said. "But it's got to be better than staying on that farm."

He said Mom had this big dream of turning the back half, the six acres that had been planted in wheat, into fields of strawberries, tomatoes, and sweet corn. Bobby would plant and manage it and get a percentage of all that they sold.

"I don't want to be a truck farmer," Bobby said.

"But you won't be," I said.

I told Bobby about the conversation between Dad and Monsignor O'Brien last March. I told him how Dad said the highway department was going to put a new road through our property and Dad and J.R. were going to build twelve houses on the back half and sell them.

"Have you said anything to anybody?" Bobby said.

I shook my head no, and Bobby nodded.

"That's between Mom and Dad. You just keep quiet and let them settle it," Bobby said.

Bobby washed his hands. He laughed as he threw the wet paper towel in the trash can.

"I will have such revenges on you both …" he added.

"What's that?" I said.

"'King Lear,'" Bobby said. "It's a play. We read it in English class. You'll have to read it one day."

"Maybe I'll read it before I get to high school," I said.

"I've got a copy in my room," Bobby said.

Bobby's bus was ready to board when we returned to Mom and Mark. Mom told Mark and me to say goodbye, and Mark started crying. Mom told me to hold Mark's hand.

She gave Bobby a kiss on the cheek. She said, "Take care of yourself," and again, you could tell she wanted to say more, but the words caught in her throat.

Bobby nodded and got on the bus. We watched him sit down at a window seat. I heard Mom catch her breath, and she took off for the bathroom inside the bus station.

Bobby gave me and Mark two thumbs up. The bus left the station.

Introit Five

What is the goal of a virtuous life?

The goal of a virtuous life is to become like God.

I drove three hundred miles because Janice said Mom was dying.

Mom rebounded however. She rebounded enough to stay alive, though like most rebounding in life, it was to a lesser height.

So on the trip to see my mother's death, we got Mom out of bed and into a wheelchair. We wheeled her to a park and a concrete picnic table. We fed her a piece of chocolate cake, most of which it ended up as crumbs on her lap. But just her trying to eat cake surprised us.

When we took her back to her hospital bed, she surprised us again.

We lifted her out of the wheelchair and onto the edge of her bed. She looked at us and said, "Are you Baptist?"

Chapter Five

Dad bought a lamb, and he bought two sows ready to litter. Dad hoped the animals would console Mom now that Bobby was gone. Of course, they couldn't. But Dad thought that maybe the animals would at least distract her from thinking about Bobby so much.

Nothing took our minds off Bobby for long, though. He had lived with his brothers and sisters all of their lives, and all of his life with Mom and Dad. He was Mom and Dad's firstborn. He would be special to them no matter what he did or what the rest of us children accomplished.

Mom talked about his birth more than the births of the rest of us, which used to embarrass Bobby. She often told how after he was born, he was colicky and cried most nights. Mom said she walked the floor of her and Dad's apartment for hours trying to get Bobby to sleep.

Like most parents, she remembered her firstborn's first birthday, first day at school, first part in a play, first everything better than she remembered anything about her other children.

So when the two oldest girls came down from their rooms in the morning, she looked to the stairway as if expecting Bobby to follow. When Mom sat down at the dinner table, she looked for him fighting for a chair among us. When Clara, with three of her younger siblings in the car, drove into the driveway home from school, Mom looked out the window expecting to see Bobby get out of the car.

Months passed before we got used to Bobby not being around, and even after his letters became more familiar than his face, occasionally, we'd forget he was gone. We'd look up expecting him to come into the house joking and horsing around with his friends trailing behind him.

Instead, we had a lamb and two sows.

Clara named the lamb Dumbbell. Janice named the red sow Lollipop. I named the brindled one Stinkeroo.

Dad and I nailed some boards together to create a sty against one side of the barn. The next morning, both sows burrowed and busted boards to get out. Dad cursed as he chased them back inside before he had to take Janice and me to his hardware store.

I helped Dad shoo Lollipop and Stinkeroo back in, but I was in no hurry to get to school. I had started the second grade, and my class didn't end up with the teacher we thought we were going to have.

Second grade was an important step in parochial school. In second grade, students made their first confessions and first communions in the spring, yet those things were on our minds as we started the first week in September after Labor Day, when school started in those days.

In those days, too, nuns came and lasted next to forever. Sister Mary Benedict taught my mother when she started grade school, and Sister Mary Benedict was still at St. James for us. She had been the principal for the last fifteen years.

Sister Mary Andrew had taught first grade for thirty years at St. James, and she would be there another twenty.

Sister Mary Louise had been at St. James for three years, and by all rights, she should have had at least another fifty years teaching second-graders at St. James.

Sister Mary Louise didn't return, though. We didn't know why. She just didn't come back. Instead, Sister Mary Maurus came.

Sister Mary Maurus wasn't young like Sister Mary Louise. She wasn't pretty. She wasn't thin. Her voice wasn't inquisitive and melodic. Sister Mary Maurus' voice was accusative, heavy and gruff. She was short, heavyset, old, and wrinkled. She wore black horn-rimmed glasses that did nothing to minimize her grumpiness, and she almost always displayed the simmering temperament of a hornet's nest – and quite frequently, one hit with a stick by a child.

She called roll as if it were an invitation to fight.

"Edward Szczykiewicz," she grumbled.

She pronounced my last name correctly. She said, "Zitch-kə-vitch." Sister Mary Benedict had gone over students' names with the new nuns before the first day because many students had Slavic names that were difficult to pronounce.

"Edward Szczykiewicz," she grumbled again.

"Here, mam," I said. "That's my name, Sister, but everybody calls me Bud."

"Why?"

"My oldest sister started calling me Bud soon after I was born. That's all I know. She never said why."

I interpreted her question as an invitation to be familiar even though her voice displayed no familiarity.

"Your name is Edward. We don't go by nicknames here."

So she called Freddy Frederick, Benji Benjamin, and Herbie Herbert.

Herbert, who was sitting across from me, reached over and poked me.

"Edward," he mocked.

"Shut up," I said and punched him.

"Edward," Sister Mary Maurus said. "You will take a front desk here by me."

She pointed her short, stubby index finger at the desk where I'd spend most of my second year in parochial school.

The injustice was that I wasn't a bad kid. My parents understood discipline, and that discipline, whether it resulted in fear or respect, molded my behavior and the behavior of my brothers and sisters unlike a few troubled children who disrupted class almost daily. They lived without fear of or respect for the nuns. The troubled kids didn't listen, they didn't do homework, and they couldn't read very well. They labored and stumbled over words and sentences as we read aloud in class, about the only class group activity in those days. The rest of us came near dropping to sleep waiting for the troubled kids to finish a two-sentence paragraph.

I could read. I could read well. My three older sisters had read to me and taught me to read. My older brother liked to read and had read to me when I was small. So I was reading before I went into the first grade.

Now Bobby challenged me to read "King Lear" when he left for the military. I was going to do it, or at least try.

So I went to Bobby's room one evening. His books were scattered where he left them. "Dr. Zhivago" and "The Brothers Karamazov" were on the floor next to his bed. I searched his bookcase for "King Lear," but couldn't find it, so I reached under the bed pulling out books that were shoved under there. I pushed some books aside and reached around. I felt the turned-over corners of a few pages touch the back of my hand. I reached up and pulled out a magazine that had been tucked between the slat of the bed and the box springs.

The magazine was a "Playboy." A buxom, blond-haired woman with her arms covering her bare breasts decorated the cover. I leafed through the pages, gazing at beaming naked women with heavy breasts and rounded, firm backsides.

The steps to the upstairs creaked. I jerked guiltily.

It had been a couple of years since Mom stopped allowing Janice to take baths with me and Mark. I wasn't allowed in the bathroom with my sisters, and women were supposed to be clothed at all times.

I rushed to put the magazine back, and once I had it back where I found it, I pretended to look at the books scattered across the floor.

The room was Clara's now that Bobby was gone, and Clara plopped down on the bed and picked at her fingernails.

"You can't come into my room without asking me first. What are you doing?"

"I'm looking for 'King Lear.' Bobby said I should read it."

Clara laughed.

"If Bobby jumped off a cliff, would you?"

"Mom says that all the time."

Clara got mad. She peered over the edge of the bed.

"I'm not Mom."

"I know. I was just saying that's what she always says."

"Well, I'm not like Mom. But just because Bobby says you should read something doesn't mean you have to do it. You're only in the second grade. You aren't going to understand Shakespeare."

"I'm not looking for Shakespeare. I want to read 'King Lear,'" I said.

"Shakespeare wrote 'King Lear,' you idiot."

"Oh," I said.

"Even if you could understand it, you wouldn't like it."

"Why?"

"Because most of Shakespeare's plays are about people with serious problems that just get worse, and almost everybody ends up getting killed at the end. That's why," Clara said.

She got up off the bed and reached into Bobby's bookcase. She pulled out a hardback book and handed it to me before plopping down on the bed again.

"I'm telling you, you won't like it."

"You've read it?" I said.

"No. We read 'Hamlet' in class. Same thing. All Shakespeare's tragedies are the same."

I was heading down the stairs when she added, "You won't understand it. You're only in the second grade, and you aren't that smart."

Clara was right. I didn't understand it. It contained more endless pride, deceit, and treachery than I had the ability to understand.

At first, I mostly read the passages that Bobby marked. One of them, the first in the play that he underlined, made sense to me several days later when Thomas stopped by. Thomas stopped a few times a week. We all liked him. He sometimes played catch or wrestled with Mark and me, and he wasn't afraid to help around the farm. He dug potatoes or picked apples when he stopped.

He was sitting at the table with us one night after supper. Janice, Thomas and I were peeling apples from trees in our garden. Mom was cooking the apples and turning them into applesauce. We already had about fifty quarts on the shelves in the basement, but Mom wasn't the kind of person who let apples rot on the trees or the ground even if she had more applesauce than her family could eat in ten years.

We were peeling the apples, Mom was stewing the peeled apples in a pot on the stove, Clara was washing dishes and Terry was wiping them. Out of the blue, Thomas asked Mom, "Mrs. Szczykiewicz, our school is having a dance this Friday night at the gym, and I was hoping that your daughter could come. It's chaperoned, and …"

"Clara's too young for a date," Mom said.

A moment of uneasiness followed, and Clara threw her dish rag in the sink. She started up the stairs.

"He wasn't talking about me, Mother."

An agonizing moment of uneasiness followed. Thomas cleared his throat.

"It's not a date, Mrs. Szczykiewicz. You'd bring Terry to school and pick her up. I understand your concern."

"No. No, you don't understand," Mom came back quickly. "I'm sorry, but my daughters don't date Baptists."

"If it's any consolation to you, I'm not a very good Baptist," Thomas said.

Mom couldn't think of anything to say to that – right away. She went into the dining room and then the living room. We could hear her talking to Dad. Mark and Dad had been watching television in the living room.

Terry never stopped wiping dishes. She wiped them with frantic energy, and only once did she look up from her wiping. She looked over at Thomas sitting between me and Janice. Thomas shrugged his shoulders, and Mom and Dad walked in the kitchen.

Dad asked Thomas to go into the next room, and Dad closed the door after they left the kitchen. We could hear a quiet discussion. Then the front door opened. We heard Thomas' car start up and motor away.

Terry started crying.

"You're too young to go on dates," Mom said.

"It wasn't a date," Terry said in halting breaths. "I've been to dances at school before. You've never said I couldn't dance with boys."

"This boy has been getting familiar with both you and Clara. He's been getting too familiar."

"You haven't said anything before."

"He's never asked you out before."

Terry started crying harder, and I thought her tears would keep her from saying anything else. But she took a deep breath and blurted, "This is so unfair. He's been nothing but kind around here. I can't believe … I can't … I hate you."

Terry threw her towel down and stomped up the stairs.

Janice and I peeled apples furiously, and Mom rattled the spoons, forks and knives in the sink. She finished the dishes and sat down with us. Mom began slicing the apples that we peeled.

"There are all kinds of boys at Christian Brothers and in our church. Why do they have to look for Protestant boys to date? I give you children everything. I do almost anything for you, and what do you say?"

"Are we done?" Janice said.

We had finished. There weren't any more unpeeled apples on the table.

"I don't know why I had any children if this is the thanks I get. I don't know why I got married. I don't know why I even wanted children. I should have been a nun."

That's what reminded me of the first line in "King Lear" that Bobby marked: "Better thou hadst not been born than not to have pleased me better."

King Lear said that about his daughters, and Lear's sentiment obviously cut across cultures and a quarter of the way around the world.

You would expect King Lear to have spoiled children, though. He was a king and his children never had to work. Everything was handed to them. Mom expected more out of us. Work was virtuous. So every day we came home, we picked more apples and dug more potatoes. We dug them, washed them, dried them and carried them into the basement where we laid them on racks in the most recessed and darkest corner under the house.

We cleaned the pig sty, shoveled manure out of Krazy Kow's stall, pulled down straw bales from the barn loft and put new straw down for pigs, cow and lamb.

Dumbbell wasn't much trouble, but she needed feeding. She browsed all day, but in the late afternoon, we gave her grain to supplement her diet of grass and hay. She grew rapidly, and soon was a stout ewe, stout enough to ride, Janice said one day.

Janice thought of it, but I was the first to try it. It really wasn't much of a ride as Dumbbell threw me off quickly. Janice and I never got much better at riding Dumbbell, and Dumbbell never got used to having us on her back.

Janice and I were the only ones who rode her. Clara and Terry were too big. Mark was too small, though he complained he wanted to try. Clara and Terry wouldn't let him, and Mom said the same too.

But for Janice and I, Dumbbell was a break from the work that we thought would end when fall came, but that work didn't end.

Dad made a deal with Mr. Williams down the road for us to glean his cornfield. So after school we dragged gunny sacks through the stalk-stubbled field, picking up ears of corn that the picker missed that we could feed Krazy Kow and the pigs over the winter.

Then we were back out in the garden and digging more potatoes, onions and turnips. Occasionally, Thomas would drive by, honk and wave. But he didn't stop now. Terry would get teary. Sometimes she would cry. Clara got angry, at first. But after the first two or three times Thomas passed, she could smile and wave too. Clara was not someone to sulk and pout for long even though she was good at it. She made friends easily, and she could find boyfriends easily, too.

I didn't have much time for my sisters' problems, though. I had my own with Sister Mary Maurus.

She sent me to the rectory and Monsignor for a spanking.

A second-grader receiving a spanking was unprecedented, and the whole thing was ridiculous. Even Monsignor said the same thing.

He said, "Well, Pat," when I showed up, "this is the most ridiculous thing I've ever heard, but we can't have students taking pot shots at the sisters with rubber bands."

That's what I had done. I shot Sister Mary Maurus with a rubber band, right in the forehead. But it wasn't my fault.

I was playing with a rubber band, stretching it across the fingers of my left hand. Of course, I was up front, just in front of Sister Mary Maurus' desk.

I was playing with the rubber band when Herbie went by my desk and knocked my elbow. My grip on the rubber band slipped and the band shot off my fingers and hit Sister Mary Maurus solidly in the forehead. She made a big deal about how it would have put out one of her eyes if she didn't have her glasses on, but the rubber band clearly struck her in the forehead and never came close to her eyes, and besides, she wore thick, horn-rimmed glasses.

She sent me directly to Monsignor. He said he believed my story, but he said disruptive students would be emboldened to do worse if he excused me. He said it wouldn't set a good precedent. So he gave me three strong whacks with his wide, wooden paddle, made me polish his shoes, and sent me back to class. Sister Mary Maurus sent a note home with me. There was no use throwing it away. The nun would see my mom at church soon enough and ask her whether I had given it to her or not.

So I handed the note to Mom when I got home, and we went to the basement with the daisy flyswatter and chair. Mom wreaked more havoc with that flyswatter than Monsignor did with his two-foot long piece of wood. Mom never asked for an explanation. She cried and said her children were going to be the death of her.

"Don't you have any respect for me or your father? Don't you understand how this hurts us? Don't you know trouble only makes more trouble?"

My punishment didn't end with the spanking. Mom sent me to bed without dinner.

I woke up the next morning starved. I heard talking in Mom and Dad's bedroom, so I went to the doorway.

Mom and Dad were still in bed. Dad knelt near the footboard of the bed. He was dressed only in his boxers, and they were slung low as if he were in the process of removing them. Mom was on her back with her legs in the air. I was still a little sleepy, so I'm not sure what I saw, but her nightgown was hiked up above her hips.

"What do you want?" Dad said.

"I'm hungry," I said.

"The food's in the kitchen, not here," Dad said.

Dad laughed as I left the room, but I could hear Mom slamming her dresser drawers and closet door.

I went into the kitchen and got a bowl of cereal. I had the feeling that I was in more trouble.

However, Mom came out in her housecoat and fixed pancakes. Dad ate and went on to work. It was a Saturday so he wasn't taking us to school. I could tell, however, it was probably best that I keep quiet about Mom and Dad's playing around in bed in the morning.

That's what I told myself. They were horsing around in bed just like Janice, Mark and I horsed around in bed sometimes.

Introit Six

How is the soul like God?

The soul is like God because it is a spirit having understanding and free will, and is destined to live forever.

Janice put Mom in a nursing home. It was too emotionally and physically taxing for Janice and her family to care for Mom. A person must be a saint to bear the load of an invalid.

But Clara was upset with Janice. Clara said that she would have taken Mom into her home. Janice said she wondered whether Clara and her family would watch over Mom as closely as they did the last time.

Clara took Mom from Janice several years ago. Clara said she had a right to have Mom part of the time, so she moved Mom. The second week Mom was there, Mom walked away. Clara's husband was supposed to be watching her, but he ended up in front of the television when Mom decided that she would take a walk to see family just as her father, Stjepan, used to take walks.

Just before dark, one of Clara's sons found Mom asleep at the edge of a road a couple of miles from their house.

Janice drove more than five hundred miles and took Mom back.

Chapter Six

DAD TOOK JANICE AND me to school in the morning on his way to work at his hardware store. Janice and I walked from the store to school. When school was over, Janice and I walked back to Dad's store, where we waited for Clara and Terry. Clara drove herself and Terry to and from the Convent, and they stopped to pick us up at the store on the way home.

A week after my rubber band trouble with Sister Mary Maurus, Clara came to pick up Janice and me. However, Dad told me to wait with him until he was ready to go home.

Something was up. Dad didn't like having us around the store. Except for Terry, we made him nervous at his business. Terry was his favorite. Sometimes she stayed and dusted the shelves and helped with the bookwork.

But this day, Clara took Terry and Janice home, leaving me with Dad. Dad gave me a bottle of soda pop from the machine out front and left me to sit in his small office at the back of the store. I watched customers come and go, and I did a little homework, some math and reading that Sister Mary Maurus assigned.

I didn't do much homework, though, because a piece of mail on Dad's desk caught my eye. The return address of the mailing showed the letter was from MODOT, the Missouri Department of Transportation. I glanced at it over and over until my curiosity got the best of me.

I picked up the already opened envelope, looked inside and pulled out a letter with a diagram of a highway and a check for a little more than three hundred dollars. The letter said the payment was for condemnation of less than an acre of land for construction of a state highway. A right of way for the road also was included in the payment.

After putting the letter back, I couldn't study.

Just before closing time, Dad came in and sat down beside me. He looked at me and smiled. He wasn't acting like himself. He fidgeted in his chair and drummed his fingers on the table.

After a long silence, he said, "You know the other morning when you came into your mother's and my room? Your mother wanted me to talk to you about it."

I didn't know why it was important Mom wanted Dad to talk to me about it.

"I was hungry. Mom sent me to bed without dinner," I said.

"I just wanted to talk to you about your mom and me."

"I'm sorry about Sister Mary Maurus. I wasn't trying to hit her with a rubber band."

"I know, Son. That's not what I wanted to talk to you about. I wanted to talk to you about, well … about women … and men. You know about men and women?"

I wasn't sure if Dad was asking a question or making a statement. I stared at him waiting for clarification.

Dad drummed his fingers a little louder.

"Son, I don't know if you've noticed, but women, when they're young girls, they don't have much shape."

Dad took a pen and drew two straight lines parallel to one another on a pad of paper.

"But as they get older their shape changes and they develop curves."

Dad drew two curved lines making an hourglass shape.

"Like this. Have you noticed that?"

"Yeah, I guess so."

I thought it would be best to agree with Dad because it seemed important to him.

"Well, that's what happens to women."

I nodded. Dad opened a drawer to his desk and pulled out a magazine that had been buried under some bills and papers.

"Now, Son, I'm going to show you something. It's not something you should look at often … or even sometimes … but it's something you're bound to see sometime in your life. Do you understand?"

Dad wanted me to answer in the affirmative, so that's what I did.

"Well, it's best you see this from me."

Dad lifted a "Playboy" onto the tabletop. He fumbled through the pages to the middle and a page that folded out. The foldout revealed three pages with one photo of a naked young woman.

"There's a reason a woman's shape changes."

Dad closed the foldout and the magazine. He stuck it back inside the drawer.

"It's so they can have children," Dad said. "I guess you're aware of that."

I knew women had children so I nodded my head yes.

"But, Son, in order for a woman to have a child, something has to happen first."

Dad looked real serious. I could tell we had gotten to the heart of our talk.

"You know where babies come from, don't you?"

I thought a minute.

"God," I said.

"Well, yes, God has something to do with it. But it takes a man and a woman to have a baby. You know that?"

I shook my head yes, again.

"They have to get married," I said.

"That's right."

Dad sighed, and he talked quickly as if he were ready for this discussion to end. He also lowered his voice as if he were afraid someone would overhear, but no one was in the store except us.

"The man has to give the woman a seed to get the baby started."

Dad's face grew even more serious.

"You know how seeds grow into fruit?" Dad said.

I nodded my head.

"Well, that's how it is with men and women. The baby can't grow until the woman gets the seed from the man."

And Dad winked.

"See?" he said.

I nodded, and waited for more. But Dad said all he was going to say.

"The woman has to get the seed from the man," I said, reiterating the point so that Dad could see I got it.

"That's right, Son. That's how it works."

Dad smiled, he closed up the store, and he drove us home. In the driveway, in the car, he paused to give a warning before we went into the house.

"Now, Son, what we talked about is between you and me. Making babies is not something you talk about in mixed company, you know, with women and children."

I nodded. I had the feeling earlier that what he told me was not to be repeated.

"That's a good boy," Dad said. "And Bud, don't say anything to anybody about the magazine."

Dad winked.

When we sat down to dinner, Mom looked at Dad. He nodded to her.

The first of October, Lollipop and Stinkeroo dropped litters. Lollipop gave birth to twelve piglets, Stinkeroo fourteen. One of Stinkeroo's was born dead, and another died a couple of days later. So they ended up with the same number in their litters.

They were cute, raucous piglets. Every day after school, Janice and I fed the pigs and ended up outside the pen watching the piglets root, butt one another, and compete for their mothers' teats.

"You know how baby pigs are made, don't you?" Janice asked me.

"Sure," I said.

"No, you don't," Janice said.

"What makes you think I don't know?"

"Because you're not very smart, and you probably haven't heard about sex. You know that's what it's called, sex?"

"Well, Dad talked to me."

I knew I made a mistake mentioning the talk with Dad, but I never liked it when Janice acted superior, especially when she called me stupid.

"What did he say?"

"He told me about babies."

"And?"

"And he told me the man has to put a seed inside the woman for her to have a baby."

Janice laughed.

"What are you laughing at?"

"That's not exactly how it works. The man doesn't put a seed in the woman. The woman has an egg and the man has to give the woman sperm to fertilize the egg."

"Well, Dad didn't say anything about eggs or … whatever. He told me about seeds."

Janice laughed some more. A person isn't supposed to hate his or her brothers or sisters, but at times, like that one for instance, a person could feel animosity close to hatred.

"You don't know anything."

I did know something that Janice didn't know, and I should have kept it to myself. But Janice's hilarity at my expense made me say what I did.

"I do too know something. Mom is going to have a baby."

"How do you know?"

"Cause I saw Dad putting a seed into Mom the other morning."

The connection between the morning that I walked in on Mom and Dad in their bedroom, Dad's talk with me about babies, and Janice's explanation all finally came together.

Janice frowned.

"It takes a month or more for a woman to know if she's pregnant. You don't know that Mom is pregnant."

"All I know is what Dad told me and what I saw," I said.

My error in judgment birthed trouble immediately. We went inside, sat down at the table, and Mom said something about Aunt Diana, one of her sisters, being pregnant.

"Bud says you're pregnant, too," Janice blurted.

Mom gave me a look of horror. Dad let out a heavy sigh and shook his head.

"He said he saw you and Dad …"

"Janice," Mom screamed, jumping up out of her chair and hitting one of the table legs so hard with one of her knees that glasses of milk splashed and plates bounced. Mom didn't go for Janice, though. She came after me with a face so furious that I was crying as she pulled me out of my chair. She dragged me across the kitchen, grabbed the flyswatter, and bounced me down the steps into the basement.

I had gotten plenty of spankings before, but none like that one. Her reproving hand and flyswatter had made me cry before, but I never cried as hard before or after as I did that time.

Mom flailed with a power I never knew she had, and I wailed with a voice I didn't recognize.

I yowled, and while I yowled, "Mom, stop, Mom, Mom," Mom bellowed that I was a worthless child, and why did she bother having a fifth child when he grew up to be an enormous dunce. She said Bobby didn't love her because he left home for the Army, and her second son didn't love her either.

"How could you humiliate me like this? How could you? How could God give me such an ignorant child?"

When Mom got done with me, we were both weak and wrecked. We had to help each other up the steps, and once we made it to the top of the stairs, she sent me straight to bed.

Usually, our house was noisy, but that night silence permeated every corner. I lay in bed listening for conversation and movement, but there was none. I dropped off for a little bit and woke up to find Dad seated on the edge of the bed.

"I'm sorry, Son," Dad said.

He patted me on the head. His hand lingered a little.

He said, "You didn't tell her about the magazine, did you?"

I shook my head no.

"That's good," he said. "Don't tell her, okay?"

I shook my head yes. Dad patted it again.

Dad started to walk out of the room, but he hesitated. He put one hand on the foot of the bed and leaned forward.

"You haven't overheard anything else we need to discuss?"

"I heard you tell Monsignor that a highway was coming through our farm and you and J.R. were going to build houses where the crops are now."

Dad sighed and came around the side of the bed and sat down next to me again.

"You haven't told anyone, have you?"

"Bobby, before he left for the Army."

Dad nodded.

"Let's keep this a secret, too. I'm going to have to break this to your mother gently. Not soon, probably not until spring, but there's no need to bring it up now."

Dad told me that he didn't want to upset Mom more than she was now.

I couldn't look at Mom the next morning. I could tell she had a difficult time looking at me. It was going to take a while before we could look at each other. We didn't have an exceptionally close emotional relationship anyway – my mother was not a demonstrative person when it came to love – but even the occasional good morning and good night kisses were gone.

A few days later, the pope died. Pope Pius XII was eighty-two years old and he had been pope for nearly twenty years. Mom was sad. Sister Mary

Maurus was devastated. Sister Mary Maurus had lived through other popes, but Pope Pius XII was her favorite. She cried when she told us about his life. She didn't like current events, but she was ready to talk about Pius.

Sister Mary Maurus told us that Pope Pius had staunchly opposed communism. You would have thought that Pius, not the United States, led the fight against the reds in Russia. She also told us about Pius' Munificentissimus Deus, which declared as dogma the Assumption of Mary, the mother of Jesus. The assumption meant that at her death, Mary was taken bodily into heaven. Pius claimed papal infallibility on the doctrine. But he didn't have to claim anything; Sister Mary Maurus would have believed anything he said.

The day Pius died, Sister Mary Maurus led my class in a rosary. That night, Mom made her family say a rosary for the dead pope.

The next day, Sister Mary Maurus made my class say another rosary, and we said a rosary every day until a new pope, John XXIII, was elected, which took nearly three weeks, from early October until late October. Once John was installed, Sister Mary Maurus quit the rosary. She replaced it with greater misery. She yelled at us for being sloppy in our handwriting – we were learning cursive. She growled if we couldn't remember the lesson from the day before, and she shook two poor students who forgot to do their homework. We thought maybe it was because she wasn't happy with the new pope. But we never knew for sure what set her off.

Mom was another matter. She grew irritable because she felt as if her authority was slipping away – Bobby left home, Terry still talked about Thomas, and I embarrassed her. We feared how Mom would reassert her authority, and we were afraid to ask for the smallest thing, such as spending some time at a friend's house or taking an afternoon off from work at the farm. We didn't dare ask to go to a movie until Mom believed she once again had control of her family.

That's why we were surprised when Mom gave in to Clara right away. Clara wanted to have a Halloween party at our house. Mom said yes without Clara having to beg or bribe. Mom was so agreeable that Terry asked if she couldn't invite a few friends, too. Mom told her that she could invite five friends;

then Terry begged Mom to let Thomas come.

Most surprising of all, Mom didn't protest at all to that. She said okay, and Terry jumped up, and hugged and kissed Mom several times. Terry said over and over that she loved Mom.

Mom said, "Oh, stop it. That's enough. Just stay where I can watch you two."

Mom told us younger children to stay out of the way Halloween night.

From the back porch, we looked in the screen door. But once a few of Clara's and Terry's friends got a look at cute, little Mark, they let us out of the backporch cage.

Janice and I went into the kitchen as the girls fought over who got to hold Mark. They took turns cuddling him and pinching and kissing his cheeks.

I wasn't cute. I was too big to hold comfortably. So they didn't bother me, except for one girl. She was one of Clara's weird friends, a noisy, heavy-set girl with a thick neck, bleached skin and a dark, little mustache. The mustache wasn't thick, just dark, which made it very noticeable.

"I like this one," she said, and she grabbed my shirt and pulled me into her lap. She kissed me and pressed her cheek against mine.

Before long, though, the girls and guys developed greater interest in music and games. They danced in the dining room and moved out onto the porch because the weather turned pleasant for the last day of October.

Clara and Mom devised a program of traditional games, such as bobbing for apples and charades. Mom had told Clara and Terry that she wouldn't stand for any monkey business, and her way of preventing monkey business was to keep them busy with other things.

But as the night slipped by, the youths tired of guessing song and movie titles. They drifted outside and chased one another through the yard. It made Mom a nervous wreck. She had made concessions and lost greater control.

Even Mark and I slipped outside. A waning, but still strong, moon cast a soft glow on the landscape, and the horseplaying youths cut shadowy figures across our yard. Mark and I drifted out to the barn. Clara's and Terry's friends were jumping off the barn fence and chasing Dumbbell around the pasture.

I told Mark that we should climb in the loft and look out the hay door so that we could see better. I went up the ladder first, with Mark close behind. When I got to the top and had my head above the opening to the loft, I could hear noises, grunts and groans. Mark hit my feet from below with his head and shoulders, and I kicked at him to hold up.

The hay loft doors for running in hay bales were open, and in the moonlight, I could see the bare bottom of a boy, jerking back and forth. He was on top of someone whose slender legs were sticking in the air. It was hard to see, but in the dim light, I knew the girl under the boy was Clara.

I started a retreat and pushed Mark down the ladder. When he started to say something, I shushed him.

Clara and her friend never heard us.

We got down the ladder, and Mark whispered, "Who was up there? What were they doing?"

I told him, "It's too complicated to explain, and you don't want to know."

Introit Seven

O most merciful Jesus, lover of souls, I pray Thee by the agony of Thy most Sacred Heart and by the sorrows of Thy Immaculate Mother, cleanse in Thy Blood the sinners of the whole world who are now in their agony and are to die this day. Amen.

The other night, Janice told me that Mom hit one of the nursing home workers. The caretaker was getting Mom out of bed to take her to breakfast. My mom thanked the nursing home worker with a slap in the face.

Who knows why.

My mom was a feisty woman most of her life.

If she thought someone needed discipline, she didn't question whether it was her responsibility to apply the needed discipline. She applied.

Chapter Seven

CLARA LEFT IN LATE January 1959.

One morning she was there. The next morning she was gone.

Mom said Clara went away to the Convent, not the Convent of the Sacred Heart High School, but the Benedictine Convent in Atchison, Kansas, about twenty miles south and just across the Missouri River. Most people knew Atchison as the hometown of Amelia Earhart. We knew it as the hometown of the Benedictine sisters.

Mom said we couldn't see Clara. She was in seclusion. Clara couldn't see anyone for six or seven months, except for the sisters, and Mom and Dad if they visited.

After the Halloween party the October before Clara left, everything had seemed better at the house. The garden work was over. We only had the animals to care for and work to do around the house.

Mom seemed happier and lighter. It wasn't as if her only purpose in life was finding jobs for us.

Thanksgiving came, then Christmas.

Bobby didn't come home, even though he had leave. He sent letters, and Mom read them at the dinner table. Mostly they were short reports, one side of a sheet of paper. He told us that the Army was interesting and he was getting stronger and more physically fit. He told us some things about his Army buddies. He told us about San Antonio, where he was stationed after finishing boot camp. He finished his letters saying that he couldn't wait to get home, but he didn't come.

He wrote me a letter once. The letter sat on the table when I came home from school. Mom told me it was there.

"Bobby wrote you a letter," she said.

When she said that, she meant, "I want to see the letter." I took it to the living room.

Bobby said that he hated the Army. He said that he couldn't wait until the day he got out, but he wasn't going to be a chicken farmer. Then he said that he cracked some drunken soldier over the head at a local bar.

Bobby was in the military police. He was a little below average in physical stature, but he said it made him feel much bigger to wear an MP armband, carry a baton and whack guys bigger than he was with the baton. He said that he was getting back at bullies for all the abuse he took from them while he was growing up.

Bobby wrote at the end of the letter that I shouldn't say anything to Mom. So I burned the letter when I took the trash out. I told Mom later, when she asked me about the letter, that Bobby only asked me about school and how the animals were. But she could tell something was in the letter that Bobby didn't want her to see.

Clara started feeling sickly in late November. Most mornings, she looked awful as she dragged herself down the stairs. Sometimes she would eat a few spoonfuls of oatmeal or a couple bites of a poached egg and then hold her hand over her mouth as if she were going to throw up. A few times she did throw up, either on the floor or in the kitchen sink. Clara missed school several times. She got behind in her work.

School went better for me.

Sister Mary Maurus let up on me. She decided I wasn't the degenerate she had thought I was. I impressed her with my math skills, and Sister Mary Maurus allowed me to move a few desks back from the front. Cyprian, one of my classmates who came over from Poland with his parents in the early 1950s, had a bad month. He lost his homework – according to him – three times, and he teased Valerie, a dull girl with uncontrollable, frizzy hair, until he made her cry. He ended up in my desk at the front by Sister Mary Maurus.

In late December, General Charles de Gaulle was elected president of France. Mom couldn't believe that any country would elect a president who had a nose as big as de Gaulle's.

A few days later, on Christmas, "The Nutcracker" was shown in color for the first time. We watched it, but in black and white. We didn't have a color television, and not many people did then. Dad said that perhaps, we could get a color set by spring or summer. He said he thought we might be better off financially then.

In early January, Fidel Castro marched into Havana. He took over the Cuban government and executed seventy-one people loyal to the former president, Fulgencio Batista. Cuba had been the second country in the world to broadcast color television shows, but with Castro's takeover, the country didn't get color transmission going again for another sixteen years.

In late January, John XXIII, announced the gathering of the Second Vatican Council in Rome later in the year. The first had been about a century before, so Catholics were excited about it – well, about everyone.

Sister Mary Maurus wasn't excited. She liked how things had gone the last couple millenniums, and especially the last two decades under Pope Pius. She said she didn't like change.

It was good she wasn't around our house. Things changed there every month or so, and that's when Clara had a long talk in the living room with Mom and Dad. Terry took Janice, Mark and me on the back porch, and Terry told us we had to stay there until Dad said we could come out.

After that, Mom and Clara didn't talk at all. Mom was testy and hypercritical toward the rest of us children, and so was Clara. If we did anything to upset Clara, such as belch at the dinner table or tell a stupid joke, Clara gave us a look that my classmates and I regularly saw on Sister Mary Maurus' face.

In late January, Clara left for the convent, and then Mom started feeling sick, too. Some mornings she was late getting out of bed, and Terry had to fix breakfast. No one, Dad, Terry or Janice, said what was wrong.

When it came time for butchering three of the hogs, though, Mom tried to tough it out.

Grandpa Stjepan walked to our farm carrying his knives with him. Dad showed up, too, but only to meet Mr. Williams, who drove his pickup to load the remaining few pigs that we weren't going to butcher. Mr. Williams took them to the stockyards. Mr. Williams had already taken fifteen pigs at different times. They were getting too big for us to take care of all of them, and Dad recouped some feed money by selling them off a few at a time. That day, Mr. Williams was going to take Stinkeroo and Lollipop to the market along with three pigs. The other three were going into our freezer.

It was a crisp morning, which is what we wanted, a cold day so that the butchered hog meat would chill and be firm enough to cut up later in the day. Grandpa wanted to scald the slaughtered hogs in a barrel of boiling water, but Dad said he didn't want to mess with heating water and scalding and scraping. He just wanted to skin the hogs.

We didn't know why he said that. He wasn't staying to help. He only helped Mr. Williams load the sows and pigs for market. Then Dad left for the hardware store.

Grandpa dropped all three pigs quickly. He came up behind them and slit their throats, one, two, three. One dropped, and two and three had no idea what happened. Two hit the ground before three could figure out he was next. Grandpa, Terry, Mom and I dragged the first hog to one of the backyard trees in which Dad had strung a rope and pulley. It was a good-sized pig, more than a couple hundred pounds.

Grandpa skinned while Mom, Terry and I tried to drag the next one to the tree. But Mom got sick from the smell of blood and lost her breakfast. She couldn't stay outside.

Thomas was passing by and happened to see us. He said he saw the commotion and the hog in the tree. Mom would have sent him home, but she wasn't outside.

So Thomas not only helped us get the two other pigs to the yard and in the tree, but he could handle a knife. Between Grandpa's and Thomas' knife skills, the three pigs were gutted and out of their skins in less than two hours and hanging in the tree chilling in the February air.

Grandpa and Thomas slit and sliced, never sawing or hacking to get through joint or knuckle.

"You have done this many times before?" Grandpa said.

"I've been hunting deer every fall since I was eight," Thomas said. "My dad makes me dress my own deer."

Thomas impressed Grandpa.

"Most young boys cannot work like this. Children are not being taught. They know little."

Grandpa stopped to admire Thomas as he wielded his knife.

"They know nothing, and nothing comes of nothing," Grandpa said with Old World gravity.

"That's a pretty obvious saying, Grandpa," Terry said.

"May be," Grandpa said. "But many people want something for nothing. They want well-behaved, hardworking children, but they do not teach them. Nothing comes of nothing may seem simple, but many people do not understand."

I was going to ask Grandpa where he heard that, but he was working on the last hog with Thomas. I knew better than to interrupt Grandpa at work.

I also had heard, or read rather, that saying before. It came from "King Lear." It was another line that Bobby underlined in his copy of the play.

When Grandpa and Thomas finished skinning, gutting and chopping off the hogs' heads, feet and tails, Thomas and I hauled the guts and skins far away from the house, near Contrary Creek.

When Dad came home from work, Dad and Grandpa cut the meat off the bone. Dad knew how to butcher. He just didn't like the dirty work of slaughtering. But he liked cutting up cold meat. We worked most of the night, cutting, packaging, and stacking the pork in our freezer. We gave some to Thomas and Grandpa.

The barnyard felt empty without the hogs. As much as we tired of feeding the sows and their pigs, we missed their robust, raucous ways.

Krazy Kow and Dumbbell seemed lost as well. They never had much to do with the pigs, but after the pigs were gone, cow and lamb paused in front of the sty and stared wistfully at the rooted and barren pen. They had no more idea what happened to the pigs than we had any idea what happened to Clara.

I wondered if Clara knew what was happening on our farm and in the world. She knew that Buddy Holly had died in a plane crash. He died in early January when a snowstorm brought down the airplane he was in. But I wondered if she knew about the Barbie doll that came out in early March. Clara was too old for Barbie dolls, but Janice wanted one, and Clara would have heard from Janice about it – if Clara had been home.

In mid-March, the Dalai Lama fled Tibet for India, and President Eisenhower signed a bill allowing Hawaii to become a state.

We didn't get any letters from Clara, and Mom and Dad didn't talk about her. Dad mentioned her and Bobby one time when he and Mom were playing pinochle with Terry and Janice.

Before Bobby and Clara left, Clara was always Dad's partner and Mom paired with Bobby for evenings of pinochle. But now Mom and Dad were left teaching Terry and Janice the card game. Janice caught on quickly, but Terry didn't like the game. It showed in her play.

Thomas was there that night watching, learning. Mom let him in after she heard about him helping us with the hogs. Mom took a hand with a ten of hearts, and Dad laid his hand on the cards as Mom started to drag them in.

"Just a minute," Dad said. "Terry, you played trump on hearts earlier. But just now, you played a heart."

"I can't do that?"

"No, you have to follow suit. You can't trump in if you have the suit in your hand that was played first."

Dad could remember every card played in a game, and he wasn't wrong very often. He flipped back through the cards from earlier hands that Mom had stacked near her. He found the hand in which Terry trumped in when she shouldn't have.

"Go ahead and play out the hand," Mom said.

In most things Mom was particular, but not at cards. She could be forgiving and generous at cards because she was a terrible player. Dad often caught her misplaying too.

"But she can't do that," Dad said.

"No, Terry, honey, you are not supposed to do that. But it's just a card game."

Mom knew how to get under Dad's skin. No card game was a just a game.

"I don't understand this game," Terry said, handing her cards to Thomas. "Here, you finish it."

"Clara never misplayed," Dad said. "Bobby either."

Terry may have been Dad's favorite, but he didn't stand for misplays in pinochle. That's when Dad mentioned Clara and Bobby – he made the comment about Clara and Bobby not misplaying, and Mom started crying, sort of. It wasn't loud sobbing, just little noises, and she took a towel that hung over the back of her chair and kept wiping her nose and eyes.

I was the only one not at the table. Mark sat on Mom's lap. Mom would hand Mark a card to play, which annoyed Dad because Mark threw the cards wildly and they ended up on the floor as much as they did on the table. I was at the kitchen counter, churning butter, shaking cream in a jar. I finished a pat of butter, put it in the refrigerator, and using a ladle, I skimmed cream off another gallon of milk.

"Thomas, I have a proposal," Mom said when she regained her composure.

"Bobby isn't here to do it, but I want to turn the back six acres into a truck farm."

I dropped the ladle. It rattled off the edge of the milk jar, the countertop and then across the floor. Everybody jumped at the noise.

Mom shot me a stern look, but didn't say anything, probably because Thomas was there. Dad stared at the tabletop.

"I'm sorry. It slipped out of my hand," I said, retrieving the ladle.

"Make sure you wash it before you skim more cream," Terry said.

"I want to raise vegetables and strawberries and sell them," Mom said. "I used to work in the tomato and strawberry fields when I was young girl."

None of us could figure why Mom wanted a truck farm. Whenever she talked to us about having to pick tomatoes and strawberries years ago, she voiced dreadful memories of long, hot days and back-aching work at ten cents an hour.

We looked at Thomas, waiting for his reply.

"Now, Mrs. Szczykiewicz, I know you have good memories of working in those fields, but those days are gone," Thomas said in a calm voice. "Food is cheap nowadays. Big farms grow huge amounts of produce and use cheap labor to get it out of the fields. You might be able to make a couple extra bucks, but the work would kill you."

If Dad or one of us had said that, Mom would have said we were trying to crush her dream. But Thomas dismissed her dream so succinctly that she was dumb.

"My dad used to farm," Thomas said, "but he turned the cornfield into pasture and raises a few cattle every year that pay for the vegetables we eat with a lot less work."

Thomas looked up from his cards.

"I'm sorry, but that's the way it is," he said. "Of course, some day, there might be a demand for local fresh vegetables, but right now, the truck farm is almost gone. You're better doing what you're doing now. Let someone farm your ground and split the profits from the crops."

We stared at Mom waiting for her to say something. She was gathering her thoughts. In the meantime, Dad dealt a new hand, and the players picked up their cards, scanning them.

It was Mom's bid. She sat there looking at the cards, but not thinking about them.

"It's your bid," Dad said.

"I know, I know," Mom said.

She moved cards around in her hand before she finally said, "One hundred and forty. Well, that might be true, Thomas. Who's ahead?"

Dad and Janice were ahead, by a lot. They played the hand out while I started shaking another jar of cream.

When the card players were on the last hand of the game, Thomas said, "You know, Mrs. Szczykiewicz, there's been talk for years of a new road splitting the valley."

The jar of cream slipped out of my hand. It hit the floor, the glass shattered, and cream splattered everywhere.

Mom shouted, "Bud, what is the matter with you?"

"Stay in your chair, Mom," Terry said getting up. "I'll help clean it up."

"You've wasted a quart of cream," Mom said.

Thomas got out of his chair, grabbed the broom and starting gathering some of the shards of glass into a pile. I picked up big pieces of glass and tossed them in the trash.

"Bud, don't move. You'll step on a piece of glass," Terry shouted.

Terry circled the mess to the drawer with towels. She threw several towels down and worked them like a mop with one foot.

Thomas swept, and he picked up the conversation where it was before I annihilated the jar.

"The state supposedly wants to run a new road through the middle of the valley, down to the end where the road heads into the hills to Dekalb. They want to do that instead of widening and straightening King Hill."

King Hill Road, which passed by the front of our property, curved sharply toward the bluffs at the city line and snaked along the foot of the hills on the east side of the valley.

"Why would they do that?" Mom said.

"Shorter road. Safer. Less curves."

"Why haven't they done it then?"

Thomas shrugged his shoulders.

"My dad said he heard the state has been contacting landowners."

Mom looked at Dad, who shrugged his shoulders and shook his head.

"Well, they aren't going through here," Mom said.

"Now, Martha," Dad said.

Dad called Mom by her name whenever he tried to calm her down.

"If the state says it's going to take property for a road, there's not much you can do about it. Are we going to finish this game?"

Dad started play on the hand that should have been over already.

"Make Bud clean up the mess. Come on back and let's finish this," he said.

"Well, how come you hear all the time about straight roads taking sudden turns?" Mom said. "Remember when we were driving to Minnesota and your friend's stinky resort? We were going through Iowa and there was that place in the highway where we took a turn and went one mile and turned again and again to go around a farmhouse."

Mom looked at Dad.

"What did you say about it?" Mom asked.

"I don't know," Dad said. "What did I say?"

"You said the people wouldn't let the road go through their place."

"Well, that's true," Dad said. "But they were somebody with influence. We don't have any influence. We tell the state they can't come across our property, and they'll laugh at us."

"That's exactly what I'll tell them," Mom said. "They aren't bringing any road across where I want to grow vegetables."

Dad glanced at me. I got the message. He didn't need to say anything.

Introit Eight

O my God! I am heartily sorry for having offended Thee, and I detest all my sins, because of Thy just punishments, but most of all because they offend Thee, my God, who are all good and deserving of all my love.

I firmly resolve, with the help of Thy grace, to sin no more and to avoid the near occasions of sin.

Janice called. She said to pray for Mom because Mom had a bad urinary infection. Janice said the nursing home was to blame. She said they didn't get Mom up enough and didn't change her diaper frequently.

The doctor who came regularly to the nursing home examined Mom. He said her kidneys and liver were failing.

Janice said she was calling the priest at her church. She said she wanted him to give Mom the last rites. She asked me and our brother and sisters what we thought – if maybe she was doing it prematurely.

I told her no, from what I understood, the last rites were for sick people, not just those near death.

But I didn't tell Janice what I really thought: If the last rites had any value, they couldn't be given soon enough. They might even have value for healthy people.

Chapter Eight

IN LATE MARCH, BEFORE Easter, which came early that year, the state highway department began surveying the new highway to DeKalb. The surveyors started about a half-mile south of the city line, where King Hill Road took its sharp turn to the east. Ribbons of yellow plastic on wooden stakes fluttered in the wind. The ribbons marked a ruler-straight line into fields and pastures, straight for our property a little less than two miles away.

Terry, Janice and I had seen the trail of yellow plastic lengthen every day during the week on our way home from school. But Mom didn't see it until Sunday on the way to church. She didn't say anything on our way into town. She just looked at the markers suspiciously.

On the way home, though, she said to Dad, "What do you know about this?"

"Nothing," Dad said. "I've seen them surveying for a few days …"

"Why didn't you say anything? Why didn't any of you tell me?"

"None of us knows what's going on. If it is a new road, I imagine I'll hear from the highway department," Dad said.

"Tell them when they come that we don't want a road on our property," Mom said.

The next day Dad came home and said he received a check from the state. He said he told state officials who came to his store that he didn't want a road, but he said they told him there wasn't anything he could do about it.

Mom cried and said it wasn't fair. She said God was punishing her for her sins and the sins of her children. She wasn't talking only about the son who joined the Army and the daughter who was hidden in the convent. She was talking about me too. I knew about the road cutting through our property. I saw the check and hid it from her. I knew about Clara and the boy in the barn loft and said nothing to her.

But like her disappointment in her children, her disappointment in the state highway department subsided enough for her to go on.

Then a few days later, the surveying of the highway seemed insignificant.

A late spring snowstorm dropped more than half a foot of snow during Holy Week. We were out of school two days. The snow covered our freshly plowed garden and the seed potatoes and the lettuce and spinach seeds we planted on St. Patrick's Day.

The morning after the storm, with school closed, we played in the snow. Grandpa Stjepan came to shovel our walk. He couldn't garden, so he brought his snow shovel and laid bare the concrete sidewalk to our front porch. Then he went to work on the driveway on the south side of our house.

Janice, Mark and I were throwing snowballs at one another when Janice stopped.

"Where's Grandpa?" she said.

I looked where Janice was looking, the driveway, and sure enough, Grandpa Stjepan wasn't there. I shrugged.

"He was just there," Janice said.

Like her, I was disappointed because I thought Grandpa left without giving us the chocolate bars that would be inside his overcoat pocket.

"Go look down the road," Janice told me.

I ran to the fence. Grandpa wasn't walking home. He wasn't on the road.

I looked the other direction, and there was Grandpa. He had fallen face first into the snowpack that he had built to the side of the drive.

"Grandpa," I said.

He didn't move.

"Something's wrong with Grandpa," I shouted. "He's laying in the snow."

Janice and Mark came. Janice took one look at Grandpa and ran, yelling all the way to the house. Mark and I stood silently on the opposite side of the fence staring at Grandpa.

Mom rushed outside in her house dress. She went through the gate and turned Grandpa over. She told Janice to call an ambulance and bring blankets.

"Papa," Mom said through tears. "Hang on, Papa. Don't go."

We learned later, though, that Grandpa Stjepan had nothing to hold onto. He was gone before he landed in the snow.

Grandpa Stjepan went to his grave in two days, on Holy Thursday, and Easter turned somber. We never found out what happened to the candy bars in Grandpa's coat pocket, and Mom didn't take us into town to the park for the Easter egg hunt.

The week following Easter, the snow had melted and surveyors hammered stakes with little flags across our property. Mom's sorrow was so deep that she said nothing about the surveyors' trail. She was oblivious to it. That wasn't like Mom. She was not a quiet person. But a pall of uncertainty came over her.

One night at the supper table, she started crying.

She said, "It was my fault. He shouldn't have been out there shoveling snow."

Dad told Mom that was ridiculous. He said Grandpa's death wasn't anybody's fault. It was just his time to go.

"He loved to work," Dad said, "and if he wasn't shoveling snow, he would have been doing something else that would have aggravated his heart."

"My sister Mary blames me," Mom said.

"She hasn't said that," Dad said.

"I know she's thinking that."

"That's ridiculous," Dad said, and he couldn't think of anything else to say that would console Mom.

Terry told Mom that God wouldn't want her blaming herself.

Mom said Terry didn't know what God was thinking.

Sister Mary Maurus remained in her despondency, too. None of us in her class knew what she was thinking. She became more irritable, and we were unable to please her. If someone left a jacket on a chair instead of hanging it up, the entire class received a lecture on responsibility. If someone forgot to do his or her homework, the entire class received an extra homework assignment and a lecture on accountability. When anyone was slow in responding to a question or someone lost his or her place in group reading, Sister Mary Maurus sighed, and said, "Jesus, Mary and Joseph," only it sounded like a curse rather than a prayer.

The whole class wished all over again that Sister Mary Louise had stayed at St. James Parochial School. If Sister Mary Louise had still been the second-grade teacher, we would have been treated much differently, and Sister Mary Louise would have been telling us what was happening in the world. She would have read from the newspaper that the National Aeronautics and Space Administration announced it had selected seven pilots to become the first U.S. astronauts. She would have informed us of the opening of the St. Lawrence Seaway. But Sister Mary Maurus only told us to shut up, sit down, and keep working.

In mid-April, Dad said that Mom was going to have another child, and that was why she was acting strangely. Terry said sometimes women get depressed instead of happy when they are having children, especially when they already have several. Terry told us we shouldn't say anything to anybody about Mom's pregnancy because they might come up to Mom sometime and say something like, "Oh, Martha, I heard the news and I'm so happy for you. You must be so happy, too."

Terry said that Mom may not act so happy. She might start crying. So I didn't say anything to Sister Mary Maurus or my classmates about my mom.

It was easy to keep the secret because my class had other things on our minds. We were approaching our First Communion, which would be preceded by our first confession. Every school day, Sister Mary Maurus recited the prayer upon entering the confessional, and we repeated it: "Bless me, Father, for I have sinned. It has been …" and there the normal penitent would tell how long it had been since his or her last confession. Of course, since we would confess for our first time, we would say, "This is my first confession."

Sister Mary Maurus went over the sins she thought we might be guilty of. She reviewed overt sins; then she emphasized energetically the sins of omission. Sister Mary Maurus said people tended to overlook the seriousness of sins of omission. She said if we failed to help someone when we could have helped them – say helping our mothers set the table – we sinned and those omissions should be confessed. She said if we knew something was going to happen that was going to hurt someone and we didn't tell them, we sinned and we should confess that too. She said if we saw someone doing something they shouldn't be doing and we failed to stop them, we sinned and we should confess it.

Sister Mary Maurus was looking directly at me. I was back at the front. I had forgotten to do a few homework assignments. At recess one day during a kickball game, I kicked the ball into a group of girls jumping rope and the ball clobbered a first-grader who was watching. The ball smacked her in the middle of the face. There were a couple of other missteps, too. I was talking in class when I shouldn't have been talking in class, and I forgot to clean up the lunch table when it was my day to be the table monitor. I even left my own lunch sack at the table.

So Sister Mary Maurus looked directly at me as she explained sin. I squirmed in my seat.

How did she know that I had kept secret from my mother the coming sale of half of our farm? How did she know that I had seen the check the Missouri Department of Transportation sent to Dad for less than an acre of ground for a highway? How did Sister Mary Maurus know that I had seen one of my sisters getting seed from a boy in high school and I didn't tell her to stop?

She told us that when we sin in word, mind or deed, bad things happen, and we were to blame for those bad things.

"And if you fail to confess them," Sister Mary Maurus said, "you have made a bad confession and that is a greater sin."

Charged and convicted, I resolved that I would tell Monsignor about my sins, my overt sins and my sins of omission.

"And …" Sister Mary Maurus continued.

I didn't want to hear more. What sinner would want to hear more?

"… if you receive your First Communion in sin, you have sinned again, and committed an even greater sin."

Sister Mary Maurus' confession education was a lesson in compounded sin.

The thought occurred to me that I would be better off if I dropped out of second grade, skipping confession and communion because I was in a hole of sin so deep that even confession could not pull me out.

However, confession was my only hope, and I resolved to make my first confession the best that I could make it. So I couldn't wait for that good Friday to come when I would enter one of those four dark boxes with the fancy wood trim, two on St. Joseph's side of the church, and two on the Mother of God's side, and heaven would pull me out of the dark abyss that I'd dug myself into.

That day came. Sister Mary Maurus lined us up, and we marched to church during the last hour of school the Friday before our First Communion Sunday.

We marched up the hill to the front of St. James Church, the bright sun forcing us to squint. Entering the church was like entering a cave. We paused in the foyer as our eyes adjusted. Then we made our way into a pew on Mary's side in front of the confessional. Monsignor already occupied his compartment.

I had been next to last in line going into church, so as the front of the line of my classmates filed into the pew, I ended up second in line for confession behind Cyprian.

Sister Mary Maurus motioned for Cyprian to go into the confessional.

All twenty-four of us watched Cyprian close the confessional door behind him. I had a sudden panic attack and wondered what Monsignor would say when he heard my sins. I wondered if Monsignor would lecture me or just give me my penance and let me go my way. I wondered how many Our Fathers and Hail Marys I would have to say for all my grievous sins.

I was wondering those things when I realized Cyprian had been inside the confessional for more than five minutes. It should have taken less than a minute for a second-grader to say he disobeyed his parents, tormented his brothers and sisters, and told white lies.

I looked up and could see that Sister Mary Maurus was thinking the same thing. She fidgeted her hands under her habit, and every now and then she pulled up the sleeve on her left arm and checked her watch. Then she looked at the back wall of church and the clock hanging over the entry doors to confirm what her watch told her.

We second-graders grew nervous because a muffled whine began coming from the confessional box. The whine grew into a high sob, and the sob grew into a child's weeping that turned into a wail. The confessional was built to muffle what was said inside, and it accomplished that. But it let noise out, and the noise it let out warped into mysterious groanings of the spirit, indistinguishable as syllables, but clear as to emotion.

In between Cyprian's howling, Monsignor's deep bass scolded him. At times, Monsignor's voice rose as loud as a rumble of thunder, and his crescendo was joined by Cyprian's wailing. Diana, one of the girls in my class, began to weep in a low voice. Sister Mary Maurus gave her a big shush, and Diana's weeping became an unbearable, repetitive catch of her breath.

Monsignor's and Cyprian's duet in lamentations reached its crescendo. The climax dropped to uncontrollable sobs from Cyprian and sharp barks from Monsignor. The confessional box door opened to the continued sobbing of Cyprian.

Cyprian didn't come back to the pew to kneel with us. He ran to the front of church and threw himself in front of the altar. He began praying the Act of Contrition in between his sobs, "Oh, my God … I am … heartily sorry … for having … offended thee …"

Sister Mary Maurus tapped me on the shoulder.

"You're next," she said.

My confession wasn't only a bad confession. It was the worst in the last two hundred years of Catholic Church history. I had all those sins to confess, but I couldn't get myself to mention one of them to Monsignor after what happened to Cyprian.

No one in class ever found out what happened between Cyprian and Monsignor. Cyprian didn't show up for First Communion on Sunday, and he didn't come to school on Monday. On Monday, Sister Mary Maurus told us that we weren't supposed to ask Cyprian about it. She never mentioned Cyprian's name, but during a math lesson, she casually mentioned that what went on in confession was between God and the penitent, and it was nobody else's business. She said it wasn't polite or proper to ask people about their confessions. Then she went back to math. We all knew it was about Cyprian, and when he showed up Tuesday, no one asked him about Friday's confession – directly.

Harold Kovelevich sat across the lunch table from Cyprian, and Harold said, "Confession wasn't too bad, was it? It went pretty fast for most of us."

Cyprian started crying, so nobody said anything to him ever again about his confession.

I never said anything to anyone else about my confession either. But mine had to be ten times worse than Cyprian's. He poured out his failings. I hid mine.

I couldn't even remember the few words I was supposed to say in the confessional.

I said, "Bless me, Father, uh, uh … uh, these are the sins, no …for I have sinned, uh …"

"Is that you, Szczykiewicz?" Monsignor said.

I had wondered whether the priest could tell who the person on the other side of the screen was. I figured he probably could, but I never would have dreamed that a priest would ask someone to verify their identity.

I said yes, it was me.

"Okay, we're running out of time. Let's move along. Tell me your sins."

I moved along with lies, well, sort of lies. I said I had been disobedient to my parents. I said I had argued and fought with my brothers and sisters. I said I didn't do my homework one day a couple of weeks ago, and I didn't listen to Sister Mary Maurus very much.

"Aren't you forgetting something?" Monsignor asked.

"What?" I said, trembling.

"Aren't you forgetting something? What about shooting Sister Mary Maurus with a rubber band?" Monsignor said. "Don't you think you ought to confess that?"

I told the monsignor that yes, I shot Mary Maurus with a rubber band.

"Sister Mary Maurus," Monsignor said.

"What?" I said.

"You said Mary Maurus, not Sister Mary Maurus."

"Oh yes, I'm sorry about that too," I said.

"I wouldn't want you to walk out of here making a bad confession your first time," he said.

Monsignor sent me out the confessional to say the Our Father, Hail Mary and Glory Be each twice.

I went back to my classmates in the pews.

I thought, "What's the use of saying the prayers?"

But realizing I needed to keep up appearances, I fell to the kneeler.

Sunday came. I made my First Communion. It was an unholy communion, and for it I received three dollars from my godmother, Aunt Bernice, and five dollars from my godfather, Uncle William. Mom bought me a rosary and a pocket Sunday missal "I Pray the Mass," which stated on the first page, "May our sacrifice ascend to Thee, O Lord, and may Thy mercy descend on us."

Introit Nine

You see me here, you gods, a poor old man,
As full of grief as age; wretched in both!
If it be you that stir these daughters' hearts
Against their father, fool me not so much
To bear it tamely; touch me with noble anger,
And let not women's weapons, water – drops,
Stain my man's cheeks! No, you unnatural hags,
I will have such revenges on you both
That all the world shall – I will do such things
What they are yet I know not, – but they shall be
The terrors of the earth.

King Lear, Act II, Scene V, Lines 272-282

Janice called and said they decided to withhold food from Mom. The doctor said feeding her only prolonged the inevitable. They gave her water so she wouldn't suffer.

Janice asked what I thought of that. I said that sounded like the best thing.

I made it to Kansas City and the nursing home in a little less than six hours. Terry, Janice and Becky were at Mom's bedside. Terry held Mom's right hand. Janice held her left.

I stayed for two days. Mom's breath came slow but regular. Her life was caught up in breathing. The doctor said he thought she would last three to four days, no more.

I drove back home to get my family. When I got home, Janice called and said Mom had died.

Chapter Nine

WE WENT TO SEE Clara a few weeks after my First Communion.

By then the transportation department was busy building the new road. The earth-moving equipment took dirt from a hillside about a mile north of us and built a road base above the surrounding farm land. Big flatbed trucks hauled in huge, long metal tubes with diameters equal to my height and dropped them in each gulley and creek that cut across the valley, including Contrary Creek. Then dump trucks dropped earth on top of the tubes.

When we got home from school, we could hear the heavy equipment straining and groaning as it dumped, pushed and leveled dirt for the roadway.

Mom listened to it all day long. She said little about the work. She looked at it suspiciously, and she worked even more diligently on the farm when it was loudest. We planted more rows of every kind of seed than we did last year even though we didn't have Bobby and Clara to do most of the work.

Our break from our own dirt work was the trip to the Benedictine Convent to see Clara – that is Mom and Dad saw Clara. Mom and Dad left us – Terry, Janice, Mark and me – on a hard bench with no back in the entrance to the main hall while they visited Clara.

Terry and Janice were in Sunday dresses, and Mark and I wore the new green suits with clip ties that we got last Easter. We didn't go to the convent just to see Clara. We also went to see a play.

Besides the convent, the Benedictines had a college for boys and a college for girls. Each spring, theater students from both schools put on a drama. That year they performed "King Lear."

We sat in the entryway while other families arrived. The theater was located in a large addition of the main building of the convent, the hall we were in. The families were not like us, with little children – at least they didn't bring them. They entered the hall with smiles and lightheartedness, while we were initially disappointed at not being able to see Clara. We were apprehensive, too, because Mom told us that we were supposed to sit down and sit still. She said that she didn't want to come back after visiting with Clara and hear from one of the sisters that we had been loud and running around. So Terry and Janice got after Mark and me for even wiggling on the hard bench.

The main building had a visitor's information station with a nun at the desk. She smiled at us a lot, but she looked too much like Sister Mary Maurus for me to trust. A family would enter, and they would stop at the desk. The smiling nun would direct them to the theater. Then she would smile at us – but mostly at Mark because he was little and cute.

Terry tried to keep Mark on her lap, but when Mom and Dad were gone for about twenty minutes, Mark got antsy. He began running down the hallway, and he ran over to the nun at the station.

"My sister is here," he told her.

"I know," the nun said. "What's your name?"

"Mark. How come we can't see Clara?"

"Well, she has to spend some time alone."

"When is she coming home?"

"Oh, in a few months," the nun said. "It won't be long. So are you all dressed up for the play?"

I joined Mark and answered for him. I told the nun yes and that I was interested in seeing "King Lear," which I had been reading. She gave me a look that said she didn't believe me. She reached across the desk and handed a piece of hard candy to Mark.

"'Nothing comes of nothing,'" I said proudly.

"What?" the nun said without a smile for me.

"'Nothing comes of nothing,'" I said. "It's a line from 'King Lear.'"

"Oh," she said. Then she turned to Mark. "Keep that in your mouth. Don't take it out so that you get sticky stuff on your nice suit."

Mom and Dad came back. Mom was sniffling. Dad, well, Dad wasn't crying. I never saw him cry, but he looked grim, like he did after the hardware store was broken into and the police called him. That was a couple of years ago, and when he came home that evening, he told us that thieves had stolen about thirty guns. Dad had a few sporting goods items, guns mostly, which the thieves had taken.

When Dad came back from seeing Clara, he looked as if something had been stolen from him.

"King Lear" didn't help Dad with his fit of melancholy. Even if he understood the story, he didn't appreciate the language. He leaned over to Mom a couple times in the First Act and said he didn't understand a thing. Mom told him to act like he enjoyed it. By the middle of the Second Act, he was nodding off.

Mark wriggled in his chair, on the floor, and in Mom's, Terry's and Janice's laps before he finally fell asleep on Dad's shoulder.

Terry and Janice liked the pageantry, and they thought the young man who played Edgar was adorable. They nudged each other every time he entered a scene.

I was enraptured with the sword fight scenes. I didn't realize in reading the play – what I read of it – how exciting they could be. The sword fights in Shakespeare were announced with the staleness of dried-out, crusty bread. For example, "Alarums. They fight. Edmund falls." Shakespeare offered no description of them. You could read past them without understanding their visual impact.

On the stage, they were two- to three-minute clashes of clacking and flashing swords. And when Cornwall and Regan ripped Gloucester's eyes out of his sockets, I developed an appreciation of Shakespeare.

Mom was disgusted with the play. She identified early with the treachery of Lear's daughters, but later she said they were too evil to be true. She believed one of her daughters could betray her, but she did not believe one of her daughters could do it so totally as to promote her mother's death. That a child would betray a parent so completely was beyond her comprehension.

She scoffed, too, at Lear's madness, attributing it to his life of ease as king and his inability to cope with aging. She especially disapproved of the young student portraying a mad Lear, showing up on stage half naked, covered by garlands.

"If he had had to work for a living, he wouldn't have gone crazy," Mom said. "Working is the only thing that keeps people from madness."

She cried, though, at the end with the death of Cordelia, as messengers arrived at the prison too late to prevent her from being hanged. Mom said Shakespeare shouldn't have written that ending.

"That's why it's a tragedy, Mom," Terry said.

"Why couldn't they put on something happy, like a Rodgers and Hammerstein musical?" Mom said.

On the way home, Janice, Mark and I lay down in the back of the station wagon. We watched the moon clip along the tops of the Missouri River bluffs as Dad drove home. We couldn't hear much over the drone of the rear tires, but at one point I heard Terry ask Mom how Clara was doing and if everything was normal.

"She's fine," Mom said. "Except it's not fine, of course."

The next week Mom got on a be-sure-your-sin-will-find-you-out kick. It probably had something to do with seeing Clara and "King Lear." She made me nervous at dinnertime with her lectures about sin never going unpunished. I knew it had something to do with Clara, but her harping made me wonder how God would get back at me for my bad confession and communion.

It didn't take long. The Thursday after the Saturday we went to see "King Lear," my day of reckoning arrived.

My class was walking double file out the school's front double doors to go to lunch, when Sister Mary Maurus stumbled. I was at the front of the line, right behind the sister with Greg Jackson to my left. It happened so quickly I never knew what caused her to stumble, whether she caught her habit on her shoe, or Greg stepped on the hem of her habit, or the wind billowed her habit so that the hem caught on the metal eyelet in the concrete that the hook on the door mated with to hold the door open. Or maybe Sister Mary Maurus stumbled over her own feet. I never knew.

But she stumbled at the top of the landing that led the first step of ten dropping to the sidewalk that took schoolchildren to the lunchroom in the basement of the church. Sister Mary Maurus stumbled, and she pitched forward, hanging on the top step for a moment struggling to keep her balance. All it would take to keep her from plunging down the steps would be for someone to grab her.

In situations like this, I usually froze, and I should have that time, but I reached out for Sister Mary Maurus. No one else was doing it. Greg Jackson didn't do it, and he was the next person closest to her. I almost had her in my grasp. I thought I had hold of her habit, but she fell away from my hand just as I touched her shoulder.

She tumbled off the top step, bounced a few times, slid down the remaining steps, and somersaulted to her back. She settled on the sidewalk in a black cloud of habit that massed around her head, exposing her underclothing, which was black too. Sister Mary Maurus quickly turned into a dynamo of flailing arms and legs that slapped and clawed at her habit to get it back where it belonged. She jumped up with the same energy that took her to the landing, and her face glowed red with embarrassment.

"He pushed her," Greg Jackson said. "Bud pushed her."

Sister Mary Maurus rushed up the stairs, so angry now that she couldn't speak.

Greg kept shouting, "Did you see that? Did you see that? Did you see Bud push Sister?"

Sister Mary Maurus grabbed me by the ear and jerked me into the principal's office, which, thank God, was near the front doors of the school or I would have lost an appendage. She shoved me onto a bench in the front room of the office while she went into the inner office and told Sister Mary Benedict that I had just shoved her down the stairs. She said she had a witness.

Sister Mary Benedict came out of her office.

"Did you push Sister Mary Maurus down the steps?"

"No, I was try…"

"No, just yes or no. Did you push Sister Mary Maurus?"

"Sister, I was trying …"

"Listen to me, young man. This is a simple question," Sister Mary Benedict said. "Did you push Sister Mary Maurus down the steps?"

I was reviewing in my mind what had happened. I reached out for Sister Mary Maurus. I felt the material of her habit in my hand. I thought I was going to save her, but maybe in reaching out to keep her from falling, I ended up pushing her just enough to send her tumbling off the top step.

"Well, I may have but …"

"Ah, ah, ah. That's all we need to know."

Sister Mary Benedict went back into her office and called Monsignor. The Monsignor came in about ten minutes later. I couldn't stand to look up. I lowered my head as he walked by. He shut the door to the inner office, and I heard the deep drumming of his voice.

He came out in a few minutes and told me to come with him. He was taking me home. I had been expelled from school.

I couldn't believe it. Public schools expelled students. They were expelled from public schools, and they came to Catholic schools where they were disciplined into social conformity or at least reluctant submission.

But I was being expelled from Catholic school.

Monsignor drove me to Dad's hardware store first. But Dad wasn't there. He had gone uptown to a wholesaler, leaving a part-time worker to watch the store. We got back in Monsignor's car. On the way to the farm, Monsignor asked me what happened. I told him.

"You are either an incredible liar or incredibly stupid," Monsignor said. "Either way, God help you."

Monsignor drove slowly, and I was hoping he would speed up – not because I wanted to get my spanking from Mom over, but because I needed to go to the bathroom. When we got to the farmhouse, I started for the bathroom, but Mom pointed in the direction of the kitchen and told me to wait there.

Monsignor talked with Mom for a few minutes in the living room. I waited with the flyswatter. I could hear the heavy equipment droning in the distance, and all I could think about was my need for the toilet.

After a few minutes, Monsignor closed the door on his way out. I heard his car start up and back out of the drive, and then Mom came into the kitchen.

She walked into the room firmly, and just as I was ready to tell her I needed to go to the bathroom, she collapsed into the chair by me. She hung her head and pressed the palms of her hands to her face. She started crying.

"I don't know what's going on. I don't know why all this is happening," Mom said between huge, heaving sobs. "Children are supposed to be a blessing from God. Blessings. They're supposed to be blessings, but all I get is heartache."

The pressure in my bladder made it difficult to concentrate or sit still. I was wriggling, and I tried for a quick apology before a request to use the bathroom.

"I'm sorry, Mom, I was just try…"

Mom came out of her chair and grabbed me by the same ear that Sister Mary Maurus had twisted. She pulled me out of the chair. She let go of my ear only to slap me across the face.

I was shocked. She had spanked me on the rear end with her hand a few times before, but mostly she used the flyswatter.

"I can't believe you children don't have any more respect for your father or me," Mom shouted. "You don't respect us. You take off, and you only think about yourselves. You date non-Catholics, and you don't want to work. And you, you try to hurt a nun, a holy woman who's devoted herself to God. What's wrong with you?"

Mom shook me, hard. She shook me, and she trembled as she shook me. I started bawling, and my bladder let loose. I could feel the warm pee trickle down my pants.

"I'm sorry, Mom, I didn't mean to push her. It was accident," I said.

"But you did, didn't you?"

I nodded my head, yes.

Mom slapped me again, and I teetered, slipping in the pee on the floor. Mom grabbed me, but she lost her grip and I fell back against the corner of the kitchen cabinet. My head sounded a loud crack. Besides a sharp pain, I felt warm blood trickle down my neck. The pain and blood forced me into making the confession I should have made a few weeks ago.

"I'm sorry, Mom. I'm sorry I didn't tell you that Clara smoked cigarettes up on the porch roof. She gave me cigarettes. I saw her that night in the barn loft, too, with that boy, and I should have told her to stop, but I didn't, and it's my fault she's not here now. And I'm sorry I never told you about Dad telling Monsignor right after we bought the farm that the highway department was going to put a road through our farm."

Mom trembled earlier, but she trembled so hard now that she couldn't stand up. She fell back against the kitchen table and collapsed into a chair, her mouth agape.

"And I heard Dad tell Monsignor that he and J.R. were going to put houses on the back half of the property once the road was in. Dad said they were going to build twelve houses, each on half an acre."

Mom's stupor deepened. Confessed, except for the "Playboys" that I forgot about as the pain in my head grew, I touched the back of my neck. When I looked at my hand, blood covered it.

Mom was looking at me, but she didn't see me.

I stood up and dashed out the back door and into the barn. I climbed into the loft and then on top of the bales of hay. I crawled into a crevice between the bales. There I finished my cry.

Introit Ten

Hail, Holy Queen, Mother of Mercy; hail, our life, our sweetness, and our hope. To thee do we cry, poor banished children of Eve; to thee do we send up our sighs, mourning and weeping in this vale of tears.

The Great Depression defined my mother's life.

When we complained that we didn't have the toys that other kids had, she said when she grew up, she and her brothers and sisters only had one rubber ball to share between them. They took turns bouncing it off the back of their house. When we said we didn't like school, she said that her education ended with the eighth grade. When we said we wanted to go to Colorado instead of spending a week in a shabby cabin by muddy Bean Lake, she said she never went on a vacation when she was a child. When we said we wanted something other than bologna sandwiches for school, she reminded us that she took brain and tongue sandwiches to school as a child and sucked on chicken necks and pig knuckles at suppertime.

You couldn't out-suffer my mother. She had suffered more than anyone in history, except for Jesus Christ, and she wasn't ashamed to describe her sufferings.

Death was a fitting close to her life, not because her restless energy deserved repose, but her sufferings did.

Chapter Ten

Mom sent Mark to look for me. He had been taking a nap in the bedroom when Monsignor brought me home. Mom woke Mark and sent him out. I heard him calling from the back yard.

Then Mark came into the barn, and he started up the ladder. He didn't climb very far. He climbed a few rungs, thought better of it because he wasn't supposed to be in the loft, and called out. When I didn't answer, he went back down and into the house.

Terry and Janice came home after Mark went inside. They came looking for me too. They climbed into the loft, but they didn't climb onto the hay bales.

"Bud really pushed Mary Maurus down the steps?" Terry asked Janice; then she called to me, "Mom said to come out from wherever you are, Bud."

"Everybody at school said he did," Janice answered. "They said Bud finally had enough from Mary Maurus. Bud, you better come out or you're going to be in big trouble."

"Janice," Terry said. "He's in big trouble already."

I didn't come out, and they didn't find me. So they went back inside. A little later, I came out from between the hay bales and peered out the loft door. Janice and Mark got in the car with Terry, and Terry drove away.

Mom came out on the back porch and stood, arms crossed, looking out the screen door. The graders and dump trucks whined and growled as they built up the new road across our property.

Dad came home early. I suspected it had something to do with my confession because that's the first thing Mom brought up when Dad met her on the back porch.

"I wanted a farm, not a housing development," Mom said. "I wanted to grow vegetables, not houses."

"We can buy a farm ten times as big as this," Dad said. "You'll get everything you wanted."

"How can I believe anything you say? You've been lying to me for more than a year."

"I was doing what was best for us," Dad pleaded.

Mom threw something at Dad. I thought it was a flower pot. I heard it crash against the siding of the house enclosed by the porch.

"That isn't going to solve anything," Dad said.

Mom screamed something, cursing maybe. I had never heard my mom curse before, so I was surprised and unsure what I heard. She went inside and Dad followed her so I couldn't hear anything else. I climbed back into the bales of hay and lay down. My head hurt, and I was so tired that I fell asleep.

Hunger drove me to the house when I woke up. The sky was beginning to lighten as I stumbled out of the bales and down the ladder. Dad's car was gone.

The back door was open. Mom was at the stove, frying bacon. I hesitated, but the smell of bacon drew me inside.

Mom didn't look up. She broke two eggs, fried them, placed them on a plate and set the plate before me. She toasted two pieces of bread, buttered and jellied them, and she set them before me too.

I ate too quickly and started hiccupping. Mom made two more pieces of toast that she brought to me along with a glass of milk. Then she got a wet washrag and cleaned the back of my head. The rough cloth agitated the tender skin around the cut. Mom put iodine on it, and my head turned to fire.

I wanted to cry out, but crying never earned any compassion from Mom, and I wasn't sure what to expect in the way of sympathy for the cut and knot on the back of my head.

Mom patted me on the shoulder.

"The garden needs hoeing."

That was my mom's way of saying she was sorry – the garden needs hoeing – that's how I knew she was sorry and I was forgiven – the garden needs hoeing. Everything was supposed to be all right.

Nothing was all right. I wanted to be like Bobby. I wanted to leave the farm, join the Army, live on a base in Texas, and whack bullies and punks over the head with an MP's authority and baton.

I wanted to be like Clara. I didn't know exactly what her situation was, but she had to be better off where she was than on the farm.

I wanted to be like Dad after the fight with Mom. He went to stay at his hardware store. He didn't come home after his workday ended. We weren't sure how long he would eat and sleep at the hardware store, but if it was a week or two, I wanted to be like him.

I was a child, though. I wasn't old enough to do anything about it. So I went to the garden and hoed. I whacked at the weeds and garden soil.

While I whacked away, I had a wish. I wished something bad on my mother. I didn't wish she would die, but I wished something bad. I didn't know what that would be. I just wanted my mom to suffer as I had suffered. I didn't pray it because praying something like that might tempt God to pay me back with greater misfortune than I already had suffered.

So I only wished it, and after I wished it, I lived in fear of my wish.

But I didn't take it back.

For a few weeks, the time that Dad stayed at the hardware store, my mother worked in the house and garden with the fervor that she had before the departures of Bobby and Clara and the building of the highway.

Mom's fervor didn't last, though.

Without Bobby and Clara, we were fighting an endless battle against nature and ourselves. Nature overwhelmed us, and our vulnerable spirits couldn't sustain us. The garden went wild with weeds despite my hoeing and the hoeing of Terry and Janice. We couldn't keep up with the reaping, and Mom lost her zeal for canning. The radishes and carrots grew old and pithy, uneatable. The beans and peas turned hard in the shell. We didn't plant corn, and we didn't plant squash or pumpkin.

We missed milking Krazy Kow a few times. She was drying up anyway, and with our help she finally went dry. One day, Mr. Williams came and loaded Krazy Kow into his truck and took her to the stockyard sale.

We thought Mom would be upset. But she accepted it silently. Her belly was swelling, and she grew more tired each day. She couldn't find the motivation for the things that once supplied her with boundless energy.

Snakes came into the yard. They mocked my mother, but she had no desire for battle.

Dad called me one night and told me he enrolled me in second grade at the rural school not far down the road. My mother didn't object.

The school had one room and two teachers. After leading students in the Pledge of Allegiance and a prayer each morning, the teachers pulled a curtain across the middle of the room. Mrs. Scott taught twelve seventh- and eighth-grade students, and Mrs. Epperson taught the twenty-three first- through sixth-graders. I was one of three second-graders.

Mrs. Epperson treated me as if I had been there all year. My reading skills impressed her. The other two second-graders weren't as far along.

One day I came home from school, and I found Mom reading a letter from Bobby. I got home first because my school was close to home. Bobby wrote that the Army was reassigning him to South Korea, to the Demilitarized Zone. Mom sat there staring at the letter for about twenty or thirty minutes, reading it over and over, until Terry and Janice arrived.

All that Mom knew about South Korea was that it was Korea, where American men had fought and died, and as far as she knew, Korea was still in the midst of a war. But as bad as that was, Mom resented something else more.

Bobby wasn't coming home on leave before he went to Korea. After he finished basic training, Mom had expected Bobby to come home for a few weeks. But he went with an Army buddy to the buddy's home in Mississippi.

Now, Bobby was being sent to Korea, and he wasn't coming home before he left.

"I know he has time off," Mom said. "I'll bet he's going with that Army buddy to Louisiana."

"Mississippi," Terry said. "His buddy's from Mississippi, not Louisiana."

"He's not coming home. That's all I know," Mom said.

Over the next few days, Mom cleaned, cooked or sewed, and suddenly she would stop and say, "He was my firstborn, and they say you spend thirty percent more time with your firstborn than any of your other children, and he can't even come home from the Army when he's on leave."

Mom was still moaning Bobby's snub when Thomas showed up and asked her if Terry could go to the Benton High School prom. That's where Thomas went to high school, Benton High School in south St. Joe. Thomas thought things were improving at our home, but he wasn't keeping up with events. He also underestimated Mom's obstinacy.

"I didn't send my children to parochial school so they could go to dances at public school," Mom said to Thomas.

She was washing dishes, and we were sitting around the kitchen table after dinner.

"Now, Mrs. Szczykiewicz," Thomas said as he smiled. "Do you know about ten girls from the Convent will be at the Benton High School prom?"

That was Thomas' ace in the hole – or so he thought.

"No, I don't know that," Mom said.

"Well, it's true," Thomas said. "She wouldn't be the only young lady from the Convent to go to the prom. Other Catholic parents let their girls date

Protestant boys."

"Well, she won't be the only young lady from the Convent or one of ten young ladies from the Convent to go to Benton's prom. She won't go."

Thomas had always been polite and patient with Mom, but he was so disappointed that his temper temporarily flared.

"Mrs. Szczykiewicz, that's just not fair."

"Life's not fair. Life's never fair," Mom came back immediately.

Mom got excited. She stopped washing dishes, and stood there with a pot half full of soapy water in her hands.

"Mrs. Szczykiewicz, nothing's going to happen," Thomas said, pressing the issue.

"You're right, nothing's going to happen," Mom said, turning toward Thomas as soapy water sloshed out of the pot. "Nothing's going to happen because nothing's going to have a chance to happen."

"You can't protect your children all your life. At some point you have to trust they'll do the right thing."

"Get out," Mom yelled, taking a step toward Thomas and waving the pot. "Get out. Don't tell me how to raise my children. Who do you think you are?"

Terry was crying, and Mark, frightened at Mom, started crying too. Thomas stomped out of the house. He didn't know why Clara left – at least I didn't think he did. If he did, he didn't believe everyone was subject to the same weakness that Clara and others were subject to. He did say, "I'm sorry," as he left the house, but Mom was still calling, "Get out," so loudly that she couldn't hear him, and Thomas was banished again from our house.

School finally ended, and we were around the house all day, but we didn't work like we did the summer before. Mom's eighth pregnancy – she had one miscarriage years earlier – was rough, and she grew much larger all over than she did when she was carrying any of us other children. She was tired and moody, so we spent most of our time outside roaming and playing. We would have enjoyed it except for knowing that something wasn't right. It was like living a life of crime and wondering every day whether this was the day you were going to get caught.

June came. Britain allowed Singapore to form a government. The United States loaded ballistic missiles on a submarine for the first time. Fidel Castro gave arms and aid to Dominican Republic rebels, who invaded the republic, trying to overthrow the dictator Rafael Trujillo. The rebels didn't do well. Trujillo was ready for them. All but four were killed.

While Trujillo put down a rebellion, Janice, Mark and I roamed freely the fields south of St. Joseph, past Contrary Creek and into the woods covering the Missouri River bluffs. Terry didn't go with us. She was too old for playing in the creek and hiking, and she was still too busy resenting not being able to go to the prom with Thomas.

We went where we wanted, and our only limitation was making sure we got back at suppertime. That meal was on the table at five forty-five, which was fifteen minutes after Dad closed up the hardware store. He still stayed at the store, but Mom remained on schedule, at least still very close to it, and habit was the only thing that kept her going.

Usually before we made it home for supper, we stopped at the house, the first one, J.R. was building on the six acres west of the highway. The crew got used to seeing us as they were picking up and putting away their tools. They teased us with the same joke every day – they said we needed to show up earlier so we could help.

We ran through the house, sliding between the studs from room to room. We picked up little blocks of wood that we took home thinking we were going to make something out of them.

J.R. stayed later than his workers, making lists of materials for the next day with a carpenter's pencil on a block of wood.

"Your dad is a very smart man," J.R. told us one day.

"Why?" Mark said.

"Because," J.R. said. "He's going to make a lot of money, and I'm going to too."

"How much?" Mark said.

"Thousands," J.R. said.

"Will it make Mom happy?" Mark said.

"It should."

J.R. paused while he licked the tip of his pencil and added an item to his list.

"She'll come around. You'll be able to move out of that old farmhouse and into a nice house."

"Are we moving into a new house?" Mark asked Janice.

"I don't think so," Janice said. "We just moved to the farmhouse a little more than a year ago."

We left the house under construction and ended up in the field by the barn with Dumbbell. Dinner wouldn't be on the table for fifteen or twenty minutes. I jumped on Dumbbell. We hadn't ridden her for months, so she was temperamental even though she was lonely without Krazy Kow and always glad to see us.

Twisting and turning, Dumbbell bucked me off quickly.

Mark wanted to ride Dumbbell then. Janice and I told him no. Mom had told us not to let him ride the lamb because Mom was sure he would get hurt. But Mark begged, saying he was getting bigger and bigger and he was big enough now. He cajoled and cried. He whined and begged. We finally relented and put him on Dumbbell.

Terry came outside, looking for us. She saw us putting Mark on Dumbbell.

Terry cried, "No," but it was too late.

The lamb jumped and bolted, and Janice and I couldn't keep up with her. Our plan had been to catch Mark as he came off Dumbbell's back since she wouldn't get far from us and Mark wouldn't last long. But she scampered from us unexpectedly, and Mark had a firm hold on each of Dumbbell's ears.

Mark screamed, but he held on until Dumbbell was about to enter the barn. Then Mark let go or he lost his grip.

Dumbbell went into the barn, but Mark slid off her back end just as she gave a little kick. So Mark did a backward flip. He hung in the air, his body rotating three-quarters of a turn so that he landed face down in one of Krazy Kow's cowpies. It was old, but the weather had been wet, so the cowpie was moist and slick.

Terry reached Mark first. His face sported a brown coating. It was in his eyes, and he was spitting manure because he landed with his mouth open, screaming.

"Why did you put him on Dumbbell?" Terry shouted.

She didn't wait for an answer. She carried Mark into the house.

Janice and I were afraid to follow Terry inside. So we stood around outside the barn looking at each other. Dumbbell came back outside and munched grass nearby.

We heard the backporch screen door slap against the jam. We figured Mom was on her way with the flyswatter.

She came all right. But she carried a double-barreled, twelve-gauge shotgun that Dad kept in his bedroom closet. She walked up to Dumbbell and pointed the gun at her.

Mom didn't know much about guns. She tried to pull the triggers, but the triggers wouldn't budge. She fiddled with the gun, until Janice told her that she had to release the safety. Mom pushed the button. Then she pulled the triggers one after another. She reeled backward from the blasts, but she didn't fall to the ground.

She dropped the gun, and she marched back to the house.

Janice turned away from me and went into the barn. I thought she went in there to cry. But she came out with two shovels. We dug a hole next to where Dumbbell lay on the ground. We hadn't dug very far when J.R. walked up. He said he'd been watching from across the road.

He looked at Dumbbell and said, "I'm going to give your dad a call."

Dad came. He picked up the shotgun that still rested on the ground where Mom dropped it, and he took the shotgun and a pistol he kept in his underwear drawer to the hardware store. Then he came back home to stay.

Introit Eleven

You think I'll weep;
No, I'll not weep:
I have full cause of weeping, but this heart
Shall break into a hundred thousand flaws
Or ere I'll weep, O fool! I shall go mad.

King Lear, Act II, Scene V, Lines 282-286

At Mom's funeral, the priest, a young priest who had known my mother only a few years, eulogized that she had been a faithful parishioner. He said he was told that my mother had sewn about half the altar cloths and banners in the church.

At the dinner afterwards in the basement of St. James Catholic Church, friends and relatives said that they would always remember our mother for her devotion to God and the church, and especially, for her solemnity.

"That Martha," Uncle William said, "she knew how to work. She wasn't afraid, either, to tell somebody they were headed for trouble."

He told us that he and his brother Stephen planned to go out one Halloween and turn over outhouses and pull other silly pranks.

"Your mother found out and she locked us in our rooms. Your mother, she wouldn't put up with any nonsense."

Chapter Eleven

CLARA CAME HOME LATE one afternoon toward the end of July. Dad brought her home. She came in the house with Dad carrying her two bags behind her. When she came into the kitchen, she took the bags from Dad and went upstairs to her room. She didn't come down until suppertime.

We sat at the table and ate in silence. Everybody was on their fifth or sixth bite when Mark said to Clara, "Why were you gone so long?"

"Did you miss me?" Clara said.

Mark nodded his head.

Clara smiled, but it wasn't her usual mischievous smile. It was a grown-up smile, a tired, beaten smile, kind of like Mom's.

"How come you went there?" Mark said.

"I was working at the convent."

"What'd you do?"

"Not much."

"Did you make any money?"

"No."

"Then why were you working? We went to the play and we talked to a sister there and she said you had to stay in your room."

Clara, who started out the conversation as if she were interested in talking to Mark, suddenly grew weary and slumped in her chair.

"How come you had to stay in a …"

"Mark, that's enough questions," Dad said.

The conversation ended, and then we noticed Mom crying. Mom gave a little gasp. Tears traced down her cheeks and dripped onto her lap and the table, so she had been crying silently a while. Her chest heaved periodically, and she made little moans.

Dad said, "It's okay, Mother. It's okay."

Terry got up and went to Mom. Terry put her hands on Mom's shoulders and began massaging them. That didn't stop Mom's tears from falling, but it silenced her moaning.

"Everything's all right, Mother," Dad said, glancing at her nervously.

That was the start of Mom's weeping.

Maybe a dozen times a week or more, she wept. We would be sitting, watching television, and she would be patching holes in socks or crocheting doilies, and she would weep. We would be driving to church or attending Mass, and she would weep. Or one time, we went to an outdoor concert at Krug Park in north St. Joe, and during the third piece by the community band, she wept so hard, we had to leave. Dad and Clara each had her by an arm and they led, and sometimes carried, her back to our station wagon.

Another time, Dad had just come home from work and dinner wasn't ready. That was a first. Mom had been married for nearly twenty years, and in twenty years dinner had never been late.

But there she was at the kitchen sink, washing dishes that hadn't even been used for a meal, and she was weeping.

Dad told her she needed to get a grip. That was the first time he'd said anything other than everything was going to be okay.

"It can't be good for the baby," Dad said.

Mom came out of her weeping.

"What do you know about babies other than how to make them?" she said. "What do you know about babies? You never fed any of them. You never changed a diaper. You never walked with any of them when they were crying, and you never read to them or sung to them in a rocking chair at night."

I don't know if any of that was true, but that's what Mom said. Dad tried to get away from her by saying, "I'm sorry, I'm sorry." He headed into the living room, but she followed him there, telling him he never went to school to talk to the nuns about how we were doing in school.

That wasn't true. I remember him going one time when Sister Mary Maurus wanted to talk to Mom and Dad about me.

Mom said Dad didn't play with us children, which was true if you didn't count the times he took us fishing or played pinochle with us.

And she said he didn't talk to us unless it was about money or something we were watching on television. That was true.

Dad took Mom outside for a walk because the argument frightened Mark and he started crying. Clara made dinner. Mom stayed outside on the porch after the walk. Dad came in and ate.

"Once the baby comes, she'll be better," he said.

The summer went that way, Mom crying, Dad saying she'd stop crying once the baby came.

Two American soldiers Charles Ovnand and Dale R. Buis were killed in action in Vietnam in late July, the first Americans to die in the conflict there. In August, the United States put Explorer 6 into orbit, and in mid-August the satellite sent the first picture of Earth from space. In late August, Hawaii joined the Union as the fiftieth state, and we went back to school.

My brothers and sisters returned to Catholic schools. I went back to the rural public school across the road. I wanted to go there and have Mrs. Epperson for a teacher for my third year. Mom didn't object. She was having a difficult time with her pregnancy and stayed in bed a lot.

Mom had her seventh child, a girl, a few weeks after school started.

Mom didn't come home right away. In those days, women who gave birth stayed in the hospital for three to five days. But Mom stayed a couple of weeks, and we didn't go to see her. Dad wouldn't let us. He said she wasn't feeling well, and she needed time to rest.

Dad did bring Rebecca, "Becky," our new sister, home the weekend after she was born. Clara took care of Becky. Clara seldom let her youngest sister out of her arms even though we all wanted to hold her – that is except for Mark. He wanted another brother and refused to have anything to do with Becky.

Because Mom didn't come home from the hospital right away, Clara stayed home from school and took care of Becky.

Dad expected Clara to cook, too, but she was so busy watching Becky, mostly carrying her around and singing to her, that Clara didn't cook. Terry fixed meals.

"You shouldn't be carrying her around so much," Dad said in the evenings to Clara. "You're going to spoil her, and then when your Mom comes home, the baby's going to want to be held all the time."

Clara didn't listen. Dad wasn't firm with her about Becky.

One day that week, I brought Mrs. Epperson and the first-graders through sixth-graders at my school to see Becky. We brought our sack lunches and ate in the kitchen. Clara dressed Becky up in a baptismal dress that Janice wore when she was a baby, and Clara showed her off with motherly affection.

That night was the first that Becky cried in the middle of the night. I heard her crying upstairs long after we all went to bed. I never slept through the night as a child. I always got up to go to the bathroom, and Becky was crying up in Clara's room. Dad let Clara put the crib in her room. I went back to bed but couldn't sleep. Soon I heard Clara come down the steps with whimpering Becky. They went into the living room. I could hear the rocker thrumming on the floor.

Becky's cries let up, but they didn't stop.

I rolled around some, then got up and walked toward the living room. It was two or three o'clock in the morning, and only a dim light from a slice of the moon came in the three side-by-side living room windows. But I could see Becky's bottle was on the coffee table, and Clara had Becky up against her breast. Clara had been singing "You Are My Sunshine."

She stopped singing and said, "I'm sorry."

I stepped into the living room. When Clara heard my footsteps, she turned Becky around in her arms and adjusted her nightgown. She reached for the bottle and put the nipple in Becky's mouth.

"What are you doing up?" Clara said.

"I heard her crying," I said and sat down on the couch.

Clara started singing again, but she stopped after a line or two.

"How come you told Mom I was smoking up on the porch roof?"

"Did she tell you I said anything else?" I said.

"What? Did you tell her anything else?"

I didn't know what to say, so I kept quiet.

"You're supposed to keep secrets to yourself," Clara said.

"I tried," I said.

"Try harder next time. Go on and go to bed."

"Okay," I said, and I stood up. But I wasn't ready to go back to bed.

"Clara," I said. "Is Dad right? Will Mom stop crying and act normal when she comes home?"

Clara didn't hesitate.

"No. No, I don't think she's going to be better. I'm afraid it's going to get worse before it gets better."

I had another question, so I sat down again.

"Clara?"

"Why don't you just go back to bed? You've got school in the morning," Clara said.

"Okay, but did you want to come back home? Bobby doesn't, I guess."

Clara's rocking picked up speed.

"No, I didn't want to come home, and as soon as I graduate next spring, I'm leaving," Clara said.

Her voice choked with her words.

"I hate this place, and I hate … I hate … Well, I don't hate anything or anybody. It's just time to leave. Go on and go to bed."

"Where are you going to go? What are you going to do?" I said.

"What are you, my parent?" Clara said.

"I was just wondering."

"And that's your big problem that gets you in trouble. But if you have to know, I'm going to California. There's somebody out there I want to find."

"Who?"

"None of your business. Go to bed," Clara said with authority. "I'm the mother here now, for a while, maybe longer. Go to bed."

I turned to go, but I still had one more question because Mom hadn't come home from the hospital with Becky.

"Clara, I need to ask you one more thing."

"Oh, for God's sake, what is your problem?"

"Can you make something bad happen to somebody by wishing it?"

"When you say you do you mean me or you because I'm wishing something for you right now?"

"Anybody," I said. "I'm talking in general."

Becky started fussing, and Clara stood up.

"See what you're doing to the baby. You don't wish trouble. You just make it."

And Clara walked out of the living room and back upstairs.

Clara was the mother for a few more days. Then Mom came home. She seemed better. She cooked, sewed, cleaned, washed our clothes and made the beds.

She took care of Becky, although she wasn't exceptionally motherly. Mom held Becky long enough to feed her, but Mom didn't pick Becky up every time she cried.

Mom didn't cry as much as she did before she had Becky, though, so we thought maybe Dad was right, and I thought Clara was wrong about Mom not getting better.

In church that fall, Monsignor made a surprising announcement. Monsignor said the Vatican, under Pope John XXIII, encouraged Catholics to read the Bible. That was something novel for Catholics. We heard passages read from the Bible during Mass, and Monsignor based his homilies on Scripture, but we weren't supposed to read the Bible. That was as startling as the news in September that the Russians sent a spacecraft to the Moon. Luna 2, a physics laboratory, was sent crashing into the Moon in the Palus Petridinis region. It did its duty. It escaped Earth and died the death designed for it on the lunar surface.

So as people on earth began exploring the surface of the Moon, Catholics began exploring a book they had often heard read from, but seldom read themselves.

The first night we read the Bible, we sat down in the living room and took turns reading five or six verses at a time from Genesis. After a couple of chapters, everyone except Mom wanted to put the Bible down and take up the television. We were satisfied with the creation and mildly titillated that Adam and Eve roamed Eden in the buff. We knew that already, but it was another thing to read it from the book it was written in.

Mom wanted to press on, however. She didn't approve of nudity, so she didn't want to leave off on a nudity note. We moved into Chapter Three, in which Adam and Eve gained clothing, and Mom was more satisfied with the state of things even though Earth, and men and women, were cursed – better a curse than nude people.

We pushed through another chapter before Mom allowed the TV to come on. Cain killed Abel, and Lamech killed two men before mankind once again called on God.

The next night we struggled through the names of Seth's descendants, we received new interest with the story of Noah, and then our interest faltered with the list of the descendants of Noah.

The third night Abraham began his sojourn and his nephew Lot was captured by enemies. That piqued some interest, but Mom was disturbed over the story of Hagar, whom Abraham took as a surrogate wife to father a son.

We had covered thousands of years of history in three nights, and we were a little weary, but Mom marched on.

Abraham became the friend of God and had his rightful heir by Sarah. The son and Abraham were circumcised, and Mark asked, "What's circumcision?"

"It's not anything you need to worry about," Mom said.

Then Sodom and Gomorrah were destroyed, Lot's wife turned into salt, and Lot's daughters lay with their father so that they would have children.

Mom was aghast.

"This is disgusting," she said. "Why did the pope want us to read this?"

She also wondered why God would put something so perverse in his book. We put the Bible down for a few nights.

That was fine with Dad and us. A new show "The Twilight Zone" had premiered on television. Mom didn't appreciate the show from the start. She had difficulty understanding the first episode in which a man hallucinates during an endurance test for what it would be like to take a spaceflight to the Moon. She didn't understand space, and she disliked being fooled by the man's hallucinations.

She also said the show would give us nightmares. Sure enough, Mark had one after the second episode. That show was about a salesman who tricks Death, who had come to claim the salesman. Instead, Death, who must take someone's soul whenever he goes looking for one, goes after a little girl in the salesman's place. A truck runs over the girl.

Mark had trouble sleeping that night. When he did fall asleep, he woke up crying.

"I had a dream Death was coming after me," Mark said. "I don't want to die."

Janice and I told him to shut up and go back to sleep, but Mom heard him and came in. His crying woke up Becky, who started crying. Before long, Mom joined in.

"I told you that show was going to keep him awake, but nobody listened to me," Mom said between sobs. "I don't know why they have to make shows like that."

Mom wouldn't let us watch the third episode of "The Twilight Zone" because of Mark's crying, and we took up the Bible again. We followed Abraham and Isaac up the mountain of sacrifice and worried that Abraham would really kill Isaac, who seemed to take the ordeal pleasantly, as if he knew the ram was caught in the thicket all along.

Dad said that if God wanted to give someone a test, it was test enough just picking up and moving halfway across a continent. Clara said the Bible was a lot like "The Twilight Zone."

Mom didn't object, but she didn't agree either.

We read on. Sarah died, Isaac got a bride, and Abraham died. Esau and Jacob were born, they didn't get along, and Jacob had to leave home because his brother threatened to kill him. Jacob's mother told him to leave home. Mom cried so hard over that we had to put the Bible away for the night.

The next day after school, I came home to find her sitting in the kitchen, at the table, sobbing. Clara, Terry, Janice and Mark wouldn't be home for about another twenty or thirty minutes. She held a towel in her hands, wringing it and weeping. Becky was in her crib crying too. I went to Becky and picked her up. She smelled awful and watery excrement showed on the back of her sleeper.

I took her to the front porch and took off all her clothes and diaper. I wiped the mess as best I could with the sleeper. I wrapped Becky in a blanket and waited on the porch until the others got home.

Clara snatched Becky from me as if I had done something to her.

"She'd still be in a dirty diaper if it wasn't for me," I said.

Terry went to Mom and put her to bed.

When Dad got home, he said he thought we needed to stop reading the Bible. He thought it was upsetting Mom.

Clara said that was a good idea. She said she had been reading ahead and we were close to a part in which Jacob's grandsons were spilling their seed instead of impregnating their dead brother's wife, and the widow ended up having sex with her father-in-law, Judah.

Dad looked at Clara and started to say something, but he shook his head, and said, "Let's play pinochle tonight."

Terry came out of the bedroom and said Mom finally had fallen asleep. Terry said Mom told her that a man had knocked on the door that afternoon and wanted to know how much she and her husband wanted for the property.

He saw the sign J.R. put up across the new highway advertising lots, and the man came to our farmhouse wanting information. But Mom thought he was asking about the farmhouse and the front six acres.

"She said she just knows you're trying to sell the house out from under her," Terry said.

"Oh, for the love of God," Dad said. "How long is this going to last?"

In mid-October 1959, Luna 3 sent back photos of the dark side of the Moon. The photos gave humans their first look at the Moon's unseen side – the side always turned away from the Earth. The Russian robot took film photos as it passed the Moon in early October, several thousand miles away. Then as the robot gravitated home, a lab on the spacecraft processed the film. In mid-October, the craft faxed about a dozen low-quality photos to Earth.

The Russians released six photos. They were shown on American television and in American magazines. Scientists were amazed at the much more scarred and pitted terrain of the dark side compared to the side facing Earth with its light seas. The flipside of the Moon exhibited a more tragic, tumultuous life.

In November, "Ben Hur" was released.

We wanted to see it, but Mom wasn't up to going anywhere except church. We told Mom that the movie was religious. We heard about it from our friends in school. They didn't say a lot about the religious parts, but they talked a lot about the chariot race, and that's the part we wanted to see.

We sulked because we couldn't go, and Mom saw us sulking, but it didn't carry any weight.

Mom was in the trough of one of her really down cycles. The low points grew progressively worse. Now she looked at us severely all the time, as if we had just done something annoying or unacceptable, and we needed reproving. It was just a look, but we knew we couldn't please her. We were too loud, or too quiet, not serious enough, or too serious.

We moved around the house as if we were walking on eggs. That's how

Clara described it. She heard the expression somewhere, brought it home, and we all started using the saying.

Mom's high-strung temperament relaxed as Thanksgiving approached. She became preoccupied with preparing Croatian food along with traditional American holiday foods. She fixed a meal that was more than adequate, and we told jokes and laughed at the table. Then we moved out to the front porch because even though winter was approaching, the weather was stuck on Indian summer. Mom, Janice and Mark sat on the swing, moving back and forth gently. The rest of us sat scattered across the porch. Dad plunked down in a metal lawn chair with his feet up on the porch railing.

We were singing and telling stories, when Mom started crying. That's the way it was – one moment up, celebrating a holiday; the next down, feeling pity, reviewing all the offenses, real and imaginary, committed against her. All of us but Mark knew, or thought we knew, what she was thinking: Dad betrayed her; Bobby hated her; Clara rejected Mom's morals; Terry insulted Mom's culture, her upbringing; I demeaned the people she respected; her husband, her own children were undermining her faith, her hope, and her love.

"You don't have to do that," Clara said.

"What do you mean 'that'?" Mom said, resurrecting her look of annoyance, impatience. "You don't have to talk to me like a child."

The porch swing picked up speed.

"I didn't mean any …"

"There's nothing wrong with me."

Clara gave a quick laugh of frustration, then she said, "I didn't say there was anything wrong with you."

"Go ahead, laugh," Mom said.

"Now, now," Dad said. "We just had a nice meal, and …"

"And what did you do to make it a nice meal?" Mom said.

The porch swing swung a little faster.

"I didn't do anything. You're right," Dad said, dropping his feet to the porch and standing up. "But I'll do the dishes."

"So you don't want to sit out here with us?"

"That's not it at all," Dad said, opening his hands to show he had no ulterior motive. "I was offering to do something."

"Something so you can leave."

Dad let his arms fall to his side, and he slumped back into his chair.

"All right, so I'll stay out here."

Mom got up off the swing.

"Well, I'm not staying out here with someone that doesn't want to be out here with me."

And she marched into the house to do the Thanksgiving dinner dishes.

For the next two weeks, Mom looked for fault with us, and generally, she found it. We'd sit down to dinner, and within two bites, Mom would say, "The meal must not be very good because nobody said anything."

She accused us of not wanting to be around her. She was right. The more she accused us of avoiding her, the more we wanted to avoid her. The more she accused us of not talking to her, the more we didn't want to talk to her. When we came home from school, we stayed outside, if it was warm, and it stayed warm into December. Or we went into our rooms and kept quiet. After supper, Dad, Mark and I left the table as quickly as we could, leaving Clara, Terry and Janice with Mom to do the dishes and take care of Becky.

If we brought a report home from school that was anything less than perfect, Mom would say, "So that's the best you can do? If you loved me, you would do your best."

It was always a question of love, or lack of it.

"If you really loved me, you would do things that please me," or "If you really loved me, you wouldn't do things that displease me."

Mom had it in for her brothers and sisters, too. We visited them once every couple months, but they never came to our house, except for right after we moved to the farm. We didn't hold it against them, but Mom did.

"It's too much trouble for them to drive a mile or two outside town," Mom said.

The only other time we saw relatives besides visits to their homes was at church.

"They say they care about me when they see me, but they don't care, or they'd come see me," Mom would whisper to us as we went into church.

Mom also exhibited strange behavior, such as leaving things in odd places. It seemed minor at first. We might find dishes or silverware left in our bedroom and our clothes on the table in the kitchen. Later though, she was putting our clothes in the trash can and dishes were showing up in the bathroom closet. She would sew things, only to rip apart the seams, sew them up again, only to take them apart once more. She washed dishes almost constantly, taking them out of the cupboards to wash them and put them back, then do it all over again.

Clara told Dad that he needed to take her to a doctor, but Dad wanted to wait a little longer.

"She'll snap out of it," he said.

Then one day I came home from school and found Mom working in the garden. The weather continued its warm pattern, reaching the fifties by mid-afternoon. Becky was lying on a blanket in a corner of the garden. On the blanket with Becky were packages of seeds left over from spring – carrots, spinach, radishes, lettuce and peas, early vegetables – but early or not, no one planted the second week of December.

"Here, Bud, help me," Mom said, when she saw me staring at her.

She stood in the middle of a small patch of the garden that she had turned over with a pitchfork. The dark, moist ground provided a deep contrast to the dried, dead weeds covering the rest of the garden.

"What are you doing?" I said.

"We've eaten the last jars of peas and carrots, and I thought I would get an early start on stocking the shelves."

Mom went back to work turning the ground.

"Your Grandpa Stjepan was supposed to come help me, but I haven't seen him," Mom said.

I didn't move. I was thinking that I should call Dad, but I didn't think I should leave Mom outside alone, either.

"Well, are you going to help me plant the garden?" Mom said.

I went to work. Of course, it wasn't fifteen or twenty minutes later that Clara, Terry, Janice and Mark arrived home from school. Clara pulled into the drive, they got out of the car, and all four of them lined up at the edge of the garden. They stared, and Clara shook her head.

"What do you think you're doing?" Clara shouted.

Mom told Clara what she had told me when I had asked the same question.

"Mother," Clara said with exasperation, and she picked up Becky before she finished what she had to say.

"Mother," Clara said. "It's the second week of December. Winter starts in a week and it's at least another twelve weeks before spring."

Clara took Becky inside, and the others followed, leaving Mom and me alone. I never stopped chopping the ground because I was afraid to look at Mom. She had started crying. Then she bawled. She sobbed. She wailed. She had no control.

I kept hoeing until finally, Mom said, "Bud, what's wrong with me? What's wrong with me?"

I dropped the hoe then. I went to Mom and took her hand. I led her into the house. She heaved and stumbled the whole way, with me doing the best I could to get her into the house and into bed. She was still in her house dress. I sat down in a chair next to her bed. Terry came in to check on Mom, but she didn't stay.

"I can't stay with her like this, Bud. I'll say a prayer," Terry said with tears running down her face.

Mom was still sobbing when Dad came home. He loaded her in the car, and she didn't object or resist. He took her to the hospital. Dad came back several hours later without her. He said she was spending the night.

Introit Twelve

Give us this day our daily bread and forgive us our debts, as we also forgive our debtors. And lead us not into temptation. But deliver us from evil.

We buried our mother in Mt. Olivet Cemetery on a blustery fall day.

Now when we get together, we tell our Mom-stories. Each of our stories is not the whole.

My mom's story is more than this story of her.

My sisters have stories about our mother that I don't or can't tell.

My brother, too.

But this is my story, though it's one I've mostly kept to myself. My mom lived another thirty-five years after we moved from the farm, but when I think of her, I remember her as she was on that farm.

My dad says he likes to remember her the way she was when he dated her. My sister Terry says she likes to remember Mom the way she was when we were all together on the porch and singing songs. My sister Janice says she likes to remember Mom when she sat in the evenings on the couch embroidering beautiful pillowcases and putting hems on fancy dresses she made.

I can't help but remember her one way.

That is my sin. My confession.

Chapter Twelve

CLARA WAS GONE THE next day. She took the suitcase that Dad was going to pack Mom's clothes in and take to the hospital. Dad asked us if we knew what happened to Clara. Terry said that before Clara left, Clara asked her if she would take care of Becky.

"But she didn't say she was leaving. I thought she was just tired of taking care of Becky," Terry said.

"Yeah, okay, but who knows where she went? If any of you know, you need to tell me," Dad said.

I felt compelled to tell Dad that Clara was on her way to California. But I'd let Clara down once before. I didn't want to do it again.

Before Christmas break arrived, I asked Mrs. Epperson at school about my dilemma. I hung around after the other students left, and Mrs. Epperson could tell something was bothering me.

"Mrs. Epperson," I said, "if someone asks you to keep a secret, and later on, someone you're supposed to obey asks you about that secret, what are you supposed to do because either way you're lying to somebody or breaking a promise you said you wouldn't break, and you're not supposed to lie or break promises?"

Mrs. Epperson said, "I was afraid you were going ask me something hard."

"You mean it's an easy question?" I said.

Mrs. Epperson laughed.

"I was being facetious," she said. "You're asking a very difficult question, and I can't answer it for you."

I told her I didn't know who else to ask.

"This isn't a math problem," she said. "This is a life problem. The rules in life aren't always a simple answer, yes or no."

"Don't the rules mean the same thing to everyone?"

"I'm going to be honest, Bud," Mrs. Epperson said. "Even adults struggle with the kind of question you're asking. The thing to remember is that even if the rules conflict that doesn't mean that suddenly there's no justice or meaning in the world."

"How do I know what to do?"

"Someone's going to get hurt. That's part of life, but you choose the path that you think will serve everyone best."

"What if it wouldn't serve anyone? Just cause problems either way?"

Mrs. Epperson smiled. She didn't say anything. She shrugged her shoulders.

"Okay," I said, and I started to leave.

"Bud," she said as I reached the door. "Whatever happens, don't blame yourself. Even if you put yourself in the predicament, don't let the decision you make ruin your life. You make a decision and go on."

Dad kept us informed about Mom's progress. She wasn't progressing. The doctor said it would be three or four weeks or more before she could come home. Dad said the doctor said Mom would act sort of funny. The doctor said the treatment would make her confused and forgetful. She might ask us the same question three or four times or more, but we were supposed to be patient and answer each time as if the question were a new one.

Mom was on our minds, but so was Christmas, which Dad did his best to provide for. He didn't have any experience, though. Mom had done the shopping in the past. When Christmas came we had a few things under a tree that Dad bought and we decorated. We opened our presents – games and sporting goods equipment that Dad purchased through wholesalers in town.

Mark and I got baseball gloves and shoes, and we each received a balsa airplane, the plain kind with a fuselage, wide wing and tail that slid together through slots made by punching out perforated sections. Plastic propellers and rubber bands powered the planes.

Mark and I tried to see whose plane flew farther, and mine usually did. When Mark complained, Dad told him that I was taller so that's why my plane went a greater distance. Dad told Mark, "You need to get higher than your brother."

So Mark was standing on the kitchen and dining room tables and winging his plane from one room to the other. Dad told Mark that was okay for a few days because Mom wasn't there, but when she came back he couldn't behave like that.

With Clara gone, again, Janice moved into Clara's room, which had been Bobby's room before he left. It was nice to have her out of the bed with Mark and me.

That Christmas night, I heard noises in the attic, so I slipped upstairs to see what the girls were doing. Terry and Becky were asleep in Terry's bed. I looked into Janice's room and she was kneeling on the floor in front of the window, which was about halfway open. I could feel cold air coming in.

"What are you doing?" Janice said.

"I couldn't sleep."

Janice was smoking. That's why she had the window open. She held the smoldering cigarette out the window and blew her puffs outside.

"What are you doing?" I said.

"Smoking. Clara left some cigarettes under the bed," Janice said. "You going to tell on me like you did Clara?"

I knelt down next to Janice.

"Maybe," I said. "It depends."

"Depends on what?" Janice said.

I said, "Depends on how nice you are to me."

"I don't have to be nice. All I have to do is make up something bad about you, and Dad'll believe me, not you."

Janice had me there. Dad always was ready to believe the girls before he believed us boys.

"Okay, I won't say anything. But I was wondering what's going on with Mom. Did Dad tell you anything more?"

"No, but I heard from Terry."

"Well,"—

"Well, do you know what kind of treatments Mom's getting?"

"No."

"Electroshock treatments," Janice said. "They strap people down and give them shocks of electricity to their brains."

"Isn't that dangerous?"

"No, stupid. They only give them low shocks. Just enough to scramble their brains but not enough to hurt them."

"Is that why the doctor said Mom would ask questions over and over?"

"Yeah," Janice said. "It wipes out people's memories. Makes them forget stuff."

"Will she remember us?"

"Of course. What do you think?" she said. "I told you they won't shock her too much. Just enough to wipe out the bad stuff."

I didn't want to talk about it anymore. I didn't understand how they could wipe out some stuff and not other things that she should remember, like her children. It didn't make sense – although events in life seemed to do the same thing to people sometime.

I started back downstairs.

"You best keep quiet," Janice said. "It'll go worse for you than me."

"I will," I said.

Mark's obsession with the model balsa airplane grew and grew. While doctors were trying to end Mom's obsession with depression, Mark's preoccupation with getting the most distance out of his toy took much of his attention. He broke a wing and the tail on his plane and robbed parts off mine. He said that I wasn't playing with it.

I kept telling him he was throwing it too hard, which made it dive straight to the floor. But he didn't listen.

He was standing on chairs and tables tossing the plane and annoying everyone. He said he was going to get on the roof of the house, and Terry said if she caught him going out Clara's window, she would spank him even harder than Mom would if she were home.

After New Year's and before we went back to school following the holiday break, Mark climbed into the barn loft. We suspected afterward that because Terry told him he couldn't go on the roof, that's why he chose the loft.

I was looking for him because Terry told me it was my job to keep track of him, but he slipped away and climbed into the loft. I came around the side of the barn when he fell out the hay bale door.

He was trying to take a little run and throw the plane, but he was bundled up against the weather and stumbled out the open door right under Mom's God's Acres sign. He flipped in mid-air and came down on his head.

He was lying on his left side, his cheek pressed into the frozen ground, his arms and legs sprawled awkwardly from his body. But his face looked peaceful, as if he were sleeping.

"Mark," I said.

He didn't move.

"Mark, you okay?"

I ran in the house and told Terry. She left Becky with Janice and ran outside without a coat.

She bent over Mark and moved his arms and legs so that he looked more comfortable. The whole time, she kept saying, "Oh, Mark. Oh, Mark."

Terry rolled him over on his back, and his head rolled much too far to the right.

"Go call an ambulance, Bud," Terry said.

As I was running into the house, Terry called, "And bring some blankets."

Janice was standing on the back porch holding Becky. She asked me how he was. I told her that he wasn't talking, and I ran to the phone. I had to look up the phone number for the ambulance service in South St. Joe that was run out of a funeral home. I had trouble telling Dixie Kirkowski, who ran the funeral home and answered the emergency number, what had happened. Dixie knew our family. She went to St. James Church, too.

She said she was sending Rob and Joe.

I went back out to the barnyard with blankets that I pulled off Mark's and my bed. Terry still squatted over Mark. She held one of Mark's hands in hers. Her other hand trembled on her knee.

She put the blankets over Mark.

"Oh, God. Oh, God, don't do this," she said. "Don't do this, God. Where are they, Bud?"

"Dixie said they were on their way," I said.

But it seemed to take forever for Rob and Joe to come. We watched as Mark's nose, eyelids and lips turned blue. Finally, we could hear the ambulance coming down King Hill Road. Terry stood up. She shivered from the cold.

Suddenly, she hunched over and threw up. Then she fainted in the barnyard.

I was standing there helpless when Rob and Joe came running with a stretcher after parking the ambulance at the end of the drive.

"What happened?" Joe said.

I couldn't answer. I looked up at the barn loft.

"Oh, Jesus," Rob said. "They fell out the door."

"I don't think the boy's alive," Joe said.

I couldn't find any words. I stuttered incoherently. They put Mark on the stretcher and loaded him in the ambulance. Then Rob picked up Terry and put her in the front seat of the ambulance, and they were gone.

Thomas had been going by as he did most afternoons. He was getting out of his car in front of the house when the two emergency workers drove away.

Thomas asked me what happened and I told him. I could find words with Thomas.

"I don't think Mark was alive," I said.

"Let's go inside," Thomas said. "It's cold."

Thomas and I sat at the kitchen table. Janice came with Becky and sat down.

"Has anybody called your father?" Thomas said.

I shook my head no and he went to the phone and made the call. He came back and sat down with us again.

"Why don't we say a prayer," Thomas said.

Before Janice or I could start a Catholic prayer, Thomas said, "Dear Heavenly Father, it doesn't look good for Mark, but we know a sparrow doesn't hit the ground but you know about it. We leave Mark in your hands, in Jesus' name, Amen."

Janice started an Our Father when Thomas finished. She said it all the way to "… but deliver us from evil," and tried to punctuate it with her amen, but Thomas added, "For thine is the kingdom, and the power and the glory, forever."

We sat mostly in silence after that. Every now and then, Thomas would say, "Dear, sweet Jesus. Dear, sweet Jesus."

Becky got fussy, and started making noise. Thomas said his refrain a few times, and the next thing we all knew, tears streamed down our faces. We were crying, but making no noise. Becky was crying, but shedding no tears.

The next day, I went to Dad and told him that Clara had gone to California. He asked me why, and I said to look for someone. He asked me who it was, and I said I didn't know, but I thought it was someone she knew at the Convent. He said thanks.

I didn't know if that helped or not, but California police found Clara in Los Angeles a week later. She had been bugging people at a Catholic adoption organization. She came home even though she had turned eighteen more than a month ago and was an adult.

Clara didn't make it for Mark's funeral. When she came home, she locked herself in her room for three days.

Bobby flew home from Korea for the funeral. He came home on crutches. He and a few buddies had been drinking and took a drive in a jeep and flipped it off a road. Bobby said he wasn't driving, and that was a good thing. He said that he had been really wasted and if he had been driving, they all would have been killed.

Mom didn't make it for the funeral. She didn't know Mark died until a week after he was buried. Dad said the doctor waited until he thought Mom could handle it and then he told her. I guessed then that meant the doctor waited until enough of her brains had been scrambled to help her deal with the loss.

Dad felt bad about Mark, but he was the kind of person who didn't dwell on bad things.

Terry blamed herself the most. She thought that when she turned Mark over, she caused the break in his brain stem. Even after the doctor said Mark couldn't have survived the fall because the break was so severe, Terry still had trouble forgiving herself.

Bobby told her she had to get over blaming herself. It wasn't healthy.

She eventually accepted that it wasn't her fault. But she needed a reason for Mark's death and she blamed Dad. We were at the dinner table one night a few days after the funeral, and Terry shouted at Dad, "How come you told him to throw the plane from a high place?"

"I didn't tell him to go into the hay loft," Dad said. "I told him to stay out of there."

We hated to think about what if Mom had been the one who told Mark that he needed to throw the plane from a high place to make it fly farther. She would have died instantly from guilt when Mark died.

We still worried that she would blame herself because she hadn't been home when the accident happened.

That didn't happen, though, right away. Mom came home from the hospital in the condition that the doctor said she would. Her eyes bore a vague look as if she had lost half of her life and personality. She forgot some things in the distant past, couldn't remember things she just did or said, and asked us the same questions over and over.

The worst part was asking about Mark. For weeks, she asked, "How come Mark didn't come home from school with you?"

But she didn't cry when we told her that Mark wasn't coming home. She gave us that blank, eerie look that Janice called the Twilight Zone look. None of us laughed when Janice said it. We said it, too. None of us ever intended it to be funny.

As much as we wanted our mother to return home a different person, this wasn't the difference we wanted. In many ways she was a child in an adult's body. The woman who once gave orders with fire in her eyes now spoke meekly. The woman who moved with assurance and purpose wandered slowly and deliberately around the house. She sat down in the evening with knitting, tatting, cross-stitching and sewing in her hands, but her fingers moved tentatively, as if they were learning to knit, tat, cross-stitch and sew, not as if they had been doing those things for forty years.

One evening as Mom embroidered pillowcases, Dad suggested we start reading the Bible again. Dad thought that might make Mom happy and give her something to talk about.

We picked up with Joseph's brothers selling him into slavery in Egypt. We thought that might upset Mom, but she took it as she did Mark's death, with emotionless resolution.

We skipped the next chapter, the one that Clara had warned Dad about last fall. Then we read about Joseph's dreams, trials and successes in Egypt until he ultimately became second only to Pharaoh. But from Mom's reaction you would have thought Joseph had only become the mayor of St. Joseph, the leader of a moderately sized Midwest town, not the ruler of millions.

Mom's apathy made me feel guilty when I thought about my wish last year. After school the next day, I stayed late to talk to Mrs. Epperson.

"Can a person make something bad happen to someone by wishing it?" I said.

"Absolutely not," Mrs. Epperson said.

She said it definitively. I couldn't but help believe her.

"You only bring bad things on people by the things you do or fail to do," Mrs. Epperson added.

I believed her, but I also didn't believe her, sort of like Terry, who blamed herself but didn't want to blame herself.

The next night we read more about Joseph and his family. A drought settled over the Middle East, and Jacob sent all but one of his sons into Egypt to buy grain from Joseph. Pharaoh had seen the drought in a dream before it arrived, but didn't know it. Joseph interpreted the dream and then took charge of putting millions of bushels of grain into storage before the drought came.

But when the brothers came to Egypt for grain, they didn't know it was Joseph who was in charge because he had been a youth when they sold him into slavery and now he was an adult dressed in Egyptian clothing and spoke Egyptian.

Joseph treated his brothers roughly when they came to him for grain because Joseph wanted to test their hearts. Joseph must have wondered after all those years how they felt about what they had done to him and if they felt remorse. They did because when Joseph mistreated them, one of them said the treatment was the result of their sin against their brother.

Bobby was home for about a month. He hung around the house some, but he spent a lot of time with his old high school buddies. They came over to our house one night, but they were too noisy and rowdy and upset Mom. Having lots of people around the house made her nervous.

Bobby said it was a good thing he was going back to South Korea. He couldn't live with us anymore.

Two nights before he left, I saw him go out to the barn. I followed him. He was sitting in the barn where months and months ago he and Bernie, Bean, and Sonny had tried to milk Krazy Kow. Bobby was smoking, something he picked up in the Army.

I sat down with him. He asked me to tell him about Mark's fall from the loft. So I told him.

"The coroner said he didn't suffer. But did he?" Bobby asked.

"I don't think so," I said.

"That's good. He was too young to die, but he was sure too young to have to suffer."

Bobby told me about Korean kids who had been burned by napalm dropped by American forces during the war.

"I wanted to hold them, but I couldn't get myself to touch them," Bobby said. "This world isn't fair. Not fair at all."

I asked Bobby if he thought Mom was going to be all right.

He said that she was going to live a long time and probably be a pain in the ass for all that time.

"The people who make life miserable for everybody live forever, and God punishes little kids," he said.

Bobby stood up. He was almost done with his cigarette. He took the butt out of his mouth and flicked it with his fingers into one of the empty stalls. The stall was full of straw.

"Bobby," I said.

I started for the stall, but Bobby grabbed me by the shoulder.

"Leave it. Let's go inside the house."

"But Bobby …"

A lazy line of smoke drifted out of the stall, growing into a cloud.

"This place wasn't meant for us," Bobby said. "Nothing comes of nothing."

We watched the barn burn down from the back porch. The rest of the family came outside and watched with us.

"I tried to put it out, but it had already gone too far," Bobby told Dad.

We were out in the country, and the city fire department didn't come because Dad didn't call them. He said by time they got there, the barn would be gone, and he didn't want to pay them to watch it burn.

So it burned to the ground, leaving only ash and twisted, blackened roof panels of galvanized sheet metal.

Two days later, Bobby left.

Even though Mrs. Epperson said I didn't cause my mother's illness, I still worried that I had somehow brought it on. So one Friday, I asked Monsignor for his opinion when I went to church with my sisters for confession. I confessed my minor sins, received my penance and timidly asked Monsignor what he thought.

"Monsignor, do you mind if I ask you a question?" I said.

"What is it?"

"Can a person make something bad happen to someone by wishing it?"

"Is that you, Szczykiewicz? What is it?"

Monsignor didn't surprise me this time asking if it was me.

"Yes, Monsignor. I was wondering if a person could cause something bad to happen to someone just because they wished it."

"Yes, certainly."

"Oh," I said, and I started to get up from the kneeler.

"But hold on, Szczykiewicz," Monsignor said. "A lot of people wish bad things, but very few of them can actually make bad things happen. Not everybody has that kind of power, and I don't think you do."

"I don't?"

"No," Monsignor said. "You didn't make Sister Mary Maurus sick."

"What?" I said confused.

"You didn't make Sister Mary Maurus sick," Monsignor said. "She had a bad heart, and that's why she had to return to the Convent. She had it for quite some time and wasn't feeling well. It wasn't because of anything you thought or wished."

I didn't know about Sister Mary Maurus. So much had been happening at our house that Janice didn't tell me that the nun had had a heart attack that almost killed her and she was sent back to Leavenworth, Kan., and the convent.

"However, it's wrong," Monsignor said. "You should never wish evil on anyone. It's a sin, and you can add three Our Fathers to your penance because of it."

"Yes, thank you, Monsignor," I said, wanting to get out of there. My confessions never did go the way they should have gone.

My mother continued to display an unnatural lack of emotion. The things that once bothered her and caused her to gripe and hound us, the leaving of clothes or a pair of shoes in the living room or the spilling of a glass of milk, drew no comment or even a sigh from her. She picked up the clothes or shoes and wiped up the milk and went about her business as if she were a maid in the house.

Eventually, though, a couple of months later, the frequency of her questions started to decline. She asked us questions once or twice, not three or four times. She told us when we were making too much noise that we were making too much noise. She told us to go to bed when we should have gone to bed, but we could still avoid bed a while because of what the treatments had done to her. If Janice was correct, that the treatments had scrambled her brains, they were starting to realign themselves. We wondered how much of the former mother we would see and how long it would take. Dad didn't know. He said the doctor couldn't say for certain either.

One day she blamed herself for Mark's death. She said it without emotion though. No tears. No grief.

"God took Mark from me because I was tested and found lacking. God gave Isaac back to Abraham because he was obedient and strong, but God took my son because I'm weak."

"Now, Mother," Dad said. "It wasn't your fault. If it was anyone's, it was mine. But these things just happen, and you can't go through life blaming yourself for them."

"They happen for a reason," Mom said.

She didn't believe that things happen for no reason. Her life was like Joseph's in the Bible. He was sold into Egypt for a purpose. Her life had a purpose too. She just couldn't see it.

One day she asked us about Mark's funeral. She had never asked about it before.

She asked Terry several times to tell her what Monsignor said about Mark and who was there. Terry told her, but Terry didn't tell her that Thomas was there. Thomas was graduating in the spring, and he was going into the Army. He was leaving right after graduation.

I saw him talking to Terry at the cemetery after the funeral. They slipped away for a few minutes into the trees at the edge of the cemetery. I followed them because I had let Clara down when she was in the hayloft, so I broke up the kissing between Thomas and Terry. It couldn't have gone much farther because it was bitterly cold.

"You shouldn't be doing that unless you're married," I told them.

Thomas laughed.

Terry said, "You mind your own business, you little creep."

She stomped away. But Thomas put his hand on my shoulder.

"You watch after your sister. I'm going to marry her when I get back."

Terry didn't tell Mom any of that. She told her at the funeral Monsignor said God has the hairs on our heads numbered, and if he notices the fall of a sparrow, he surely notices the fall of a young child, someone of much more value than many sparrows.

Mom liked the reference to sparrows. It gave her comfort to look out the window at the birds picking through the dead and deteriorating plants and weeds of our garden. She asked Dad to bring home bird seed, and she scattered it so that cardinals, sparrows, juncos and mourning doves were picking through our garden most of the day.

Eventually though, the cooing doves, peeping sparrows and whistling cardinals were run off by blackbirds – grackles, starlings, cowbirds – that flocked in huge noisy numbers. They scared Mom. She said that her dad believed blackbirds were bad luck. So she stopped putting out seed, and the half-empty bag of seed sat on the back porch until mice found it, and Dad had to haul it away.

In January 1960, John Kennedy announced that he would run for president. Dad liked him because he was a Democrat and Catholic, but Dad thought Kennedy was too young to run for president.

In February, four black college students sat down at a segregated Woolworth's lunch counter in North Carolina and refused to leave.

At the end of the month, France tested a nuclear bomb in the Sahara Desert.

In early March, President Eisenhower said he would send three thousand five hundred American troops to Vietnam. Dad said that place was going to be another Korea.

"How do you know?" Clara said. "You don't even know where Vietnam is."

"We ought to stay out of their troubles. We've got our own."

We read from Genesis sporadically, but one mid-March night we wrapped up the book. Joseph revealed himself to his brothers and was reunited with his father, Jacob, and the rest of his family. They all came to Egypt, and Jacob and his family prospered there.

But not long after, Jacob died. The brothers, afraid that Joseph would now repay them for the evil they did to him, begged his forgiveness.

Joseph told his brothers that they meant evil, but God meant good by what they had done. Then Joseph died and told his family to carry his bones back to Israel when they returned, whenever that was.

We sat in the living room of the farmhouse, most of us proud that we had made it through the first book of the Bible, even if it took months.

Mom turned to Dad.

She said, "I don't want to stay here anymore."

"What?" Dad said.

"I don't want to stay here anymore," Mom said. "I don't want to live here anymore."

"Are you sure?" Dad said.

Mom told him she was sure.

Dad figured the day was coming, and he had bought a house in town without telling any of us.

Clara said Mom finally came to her senses.

"We didn't belong here from the start, not just since Mom started losing it," Clara said. "Thank God for modern medicine. She never would have lasted through this place and Mark's death without it."

So we moved into town. We moved the next day into a big, two-story house, in which each of us had our own bedroom. Mom sat in the kitchen in a hard-backed chair while we moved everything inside. When we were done, she got up and went to bed.

We were worried about the next morning, but she fixed breakfast when she woke up and started arranging things. She never mentioned the farm that day or any day after until she developed Alzheimer's.

Mom regained most of her fire. She cried again, the first time a year later when Clara got married. She disciplined again, too. Discipline was ingrained in her, and it couldn't be erased so easily. But the later discipline lacked her earlier passion and energy.

She never raised a chicken, hog, cow or calf again; never raised strawberries, corn, squash, beans or any other vegetable again; never filled a basement with canned goods or potatoes again. She bought them at the grocery store.

The only gardening she did was to raise marigolds and geraniums in planters and pots around the yard of our house in town. I helped Mom each spring until I was eighteen. Then I moved away, and I always kept at least three hundred miles between me and my mom and the marigolds and geraniums.

Dad sold the farm, the front six acres with the farmhouse about two weeks after we moved. In the next three years, he and J.R. sold twelve new houses on the back half of the farm. They called the addition "Easy Acres."

When the last of the twelve houses sold, Dad said, "I knew when I bought that twelve acres it was prime property and it'd turn out good."

ABOUT THE AUTHOR

David Gerard was born David Gerard Jurkiewicz in 1952 in St. Joseph, Missouri. He attended parochial schools there and, as a youth, worked in his father's shoe repair business. He earned a Master's degree in literature from the University of Tulsa in 1992. He has worked for the Muskogee Phoenix in Muskogee, Oklahoma, since 1995 where he spent ten years as a reporter and copy editor and the last five years as opinion editor. He is a freelance writer, has written two other novels, *Judge Not* and *The Nightwalker's Lament,* and a few of his short stories have been published in literary magazines. Gerard and his wife Audrey have three adult children. He enjoys gardening, hiking, bicycling, and birdwatching.

CPSIA information can be obtained
at www.ICGtesting.com
Printed in the USA
BVHW082245170521
607554BV00007B/1468